The Mystery of Meditation

Emmanuel Adewusi

CCCG Publishing House

Copyright © 2024 Emmanuel Adewusi

All rights reserved. No part of this book may be used or reproduced by any means, graphics, electronic, or mechanical, including photocopying, recording, taping, or by any information storage retrieval system without the author's written permission except in cases of brief quotations embodied in critical articles and reviews.

Scriptures are taken from the New King James Version. Copyright 1979, 1980, 1982 by Thomas Nelson, Inc. Used by permission. All right reserved.

Author: Emmanuel Adewusi

ISBN: 978-1-989099-32-2 (hardcover)

ISBN: 978-1-989099-33-9 (ebook)

First Printing 2024

Contents

Dedication	IV
Preface	V
Introduction	VII
1. What is Meditation?	1
2. Benefits of Meditation	14
3. Christian Meditation Approaches	33
4. Mysteries of Darkness	48
5. Distractions in Meditation	62
6. Meditation Tools	83
7. Frequently Asked Questions	99
Epilogue	109
Contact the Author	111
A Sinner's Prayer	112
About the Author	113

Dedication

To Jesus Christ, the Chief Cornerstone, and the Head of the church, whose teachings and example illuminate the path of enlightenment and inner peace.

This book is dedicated to all embarking on the journey to rediscover the ancient art of meditation and to reintegrate it into the spiritual fabric of the body of Christ. May your pursuit be guided by His wisdom and grace, leading you to profound insights, transformative experiences, and a deeper communion with the Holy Spirit.

May the pages within serve as a beacon of light, illuminating the mysteries of meditation and inspiring you to cultivate a sacred space within your heart where you can commune with the presence of the Almighty God.

Preface

WHY WRITE ANOTHER BOOK ON MEDITATION?

If you explore any bookstore globally today, you will discover an abundance of books on meditation. Similarly, if you visit any store selling magazines, you will encounter numerous titles covering meditation, spirituality, manifestation, methods to quiet the mind, and much more.

As I learn and practice meditation, I realize that not all meditation is the same. Just as not every food is beneficial for the body, Christians should not partake in just any meditative practice they come across. I decided to write this book and launch the Hour of Meditation (HoM) on my YouTube Channel (@Emmanuel Adewusi) after receiving marching orders from God.

There is hardly any successful person I have met, read about, or heard of who does not engage in some form of meditative practice. It seems almost impossible to operate at the forefront of innovation and excellence if all one does is reiterate what others have already said. Meditation enables us to connect more deeply with our past, present, and future selves, surroundings, and God.

Although meditation, quietness, manifestation, and other similar terms are widely known, many need help understanding the mechanics of meditation correctly. This book and HoM sessions aim to guide you into the deeper realms of meditation, along with all its attendant blessings.

Introduction

Let me share three stories that inspired me to write this book. The first story is about a Christian who does not understand meditation and, as a result, has ignorantly engaged in it. Let's refer to this Christian as Donald. The second story involves a Christian who has heard of meditation but is more acquainted with its dangers, leading to a profound fear of anything related to meditation. We'll call this cautious Christian, Dave. The third story is about a Christian who recognizes the benefits of meditation but is also mindful of its dangers. This knowledgeable Christian will be named Donna.

THE IGNORANT CHRISTIAN

Donald was raised in a typical American Christian household where attending church was common yet not mandatory. His upbringing instilled in him the belief that, while Christianity was the preferred faith of his family, other religions were also valid and warranted exploration. Donald's approach to faith was non-judgmental, embodying a liberal perspective. Upon encountering yoga during his university years, he was intrigued and decided to give it a try. What began as a casual involvement deepened as he found certain aspects of yoga to be grounding, leading him to explore further.

In his quest, Donald discovered a variety of meditation audios that drew upon Hindu and Buddhist philosophies. He found these guided audios appealing for their practicality, and soon, reciting the chants became a habitual part of his routine. Over time, he developed a keen interest in chakras and energy transference concepts. As his engagement with meditative yoga practices intensified, so did the frequency of his unusual spiritual experiences. Unbeknownst to him, these were linked to his yoga practices.

Donald represents a growing faction of Christians who, despite identifying with the Christian faith, fail to recognize the implications of dabbling in spiritual practices from other religions. Such engagements can inadvertently grant access to the entities associated with those religions. Many modern-day Christians are lured by the initial innocence of these practices, not realizing the potential spiritual consequences. While Christians typically extend overt invitations for others to come to know Christ, proponents of other faiths might employ more subtle methods, drawing people into their folds through seemingly harmless activities until they are fully integrated.

As for Donald, without realizing the potential implications of his spiritual explorations, he risks drifting away from his Christian faith, experiencing spiritual turmoil, or becoming ensnared in practices that conflict with his initial beliefs.

THE FEARFUL CHRISTIAN

Dave was raised in a very strict Christian family where not only was regular church attendance mandatory, but active service within their church community was also expected. From a young age, Dave was taught to view all spiritual matters with suspicion. He holds a belief in the omnipotence of God yet harbours a deep-seated fear of demons, having witnessed numerous instances where demons were cast out of individuals. These experiences led him to vow never to find himself in such a predicament. Deliverance services at his church evoke a mix of excitement and trepidation in Dave, especially the anxiety regarding the notion that one might "catch" a demon in a manner akin to contracting the COVID-19 virus. Dave tends to interpret every unfortunate and unexplained incident as an indication of demonic activity. Consequently, when his pastor highlighted the dangers associated with yoga, Dave immediately vowed to steer clear of meditation altogether.

Dave represents a growing number of Christians who, due to their fears, overlook the potential benefits of meditation. While it's true that, much like fire, meditation can be harmful if not approached correctly, it's important to acknowledge that, with the right guidance, it's possible to engage in meditation safely without inviting negative spiritual consequences. Despite his justifiable concerns, Dave simply requires access to resources that can teach him how to meditate in a manner that aligns with his faith and safeguards against the spiritual dangers he fears so deeply.

THE INFORMED CHRISTIAN

Donna represents the type of Christian we should all aspire to become. I sincerely hope and desire that by reading this book, you will become informed about meditation in the way Donna has. She recognizes that meditation is not only a fundamental Christian practice but is also aware of the dangers associated with practicing it improperly. Rather than shying away from meditation, she responded like the Berean Christians in Acts 17 and sought accurate information. Since a resource like this book was unavailable to her, she relied on watching videos and asking knowledgeable individuals pertinent questions. Through diligent study, she discovered the proper boundaries of ideal Christian meditative practices and has consistently grown in understanding and applying these practices.

Donna skillfully incorporates meditation into her everyday life, utilizing various techniques depending on her specific goals. Moreover, she knows how to overcome common obstacles that hinder effective meditation.

Whether you relate to Dave, Donald, Donna, or perhaps somewhere in between, this book aims to equip you with sufficient information to dispel any fears and correct any misconceptions regarding meditation.

1
What is Meditation?

Perhaps your first question is, what exactly is meditation? Meditation means different things to different people. To some, meditation is simply the art of being grounded, centred, or mindful through quietness or focused observation. To others, meditation is about the art of creation through visualization. Yet, to others, it is repeating a phrase (mantra) until the practitioner ceases to be aware of their environment. To a small group of fervent adherents, there is an understanding that meditation is the process of giving a spiritual entity access to your body, soul, and/or spirit.

When you combine all these descriptions of meditation, you will understand the benefits and potential dangers of meditation. The practices involved in meditation are typically the same regardless of the end result. In essence, whether your meditation is meant for channelling demonic spirits or the Holy Spirit, it will not change the core techniques you apply.

Meditation is an opportunity to come into agreement with divinity. It allows us to deal with deep things within ourselves. If we don't meditate, we are left with shallow things. Gold is so valuable that it is not found on the surface but deep in the ground. I will show you how meditation can facilitate agreement and, subsequently, the release of powerful virtues. Get ready for an exciting moment of deliverance, freedom, and learning.

Several key components characterize meditation:

- Assuming a posture of humility mentally, emotionally, and physically in order to be filled with God.

- The intentional act of travelling into the future while remaining in the present.

- The accurate management of our inner life.

- Retreating to listen with your inner ears or retreating to see with your inner eyes.

- The art of waiting on the Lord (Isaiah 40:31)

- Keeping quiet so we can gain confidence (Isaiah 30:15)

- The process of alignment by pondering the path of our feet: the effort we engage in to align our soul, mind, will and emotions to our spirit (Proverbs 4:26)

- Being still so we can know God (Psalms 46:10)

- Searching for the voice of God (1 Kings 19:11). Elijah was searching for the Lord, not for the by-products of God, which were displayed as the wind, earthquake and fire. When we meditate, we aim to find God and hold on until the word comes.

What, then, are the major differences between godly and ungodly meditation?

Non-Christian Meditation

The primary objective of non-Christian meditation is to elevate the self or entities other than the Holy Spirit. Examples of secular meditation include yoga, hypnosis, manifestation, and channelling. These meditation types adopt practices with Biblical roots but lack submission to the will of the Holy Spirit and Jesus Christ.

In yoga, the goal is for the practitioner to reach a specific place, state, time, or a combination thereof. Non-Christian meditation utilizes quietness (stillness), affirmations (chants), space (energy source), posture, substances (psychedelic drugs), sound (sacred frequencies), and the word (sacred texts). Most yoga practitioners start with quietness and perhaps affirmations, while deeper practitioners engage with sacred spaces, frequencies, texts, etc. Yoga and other secular meditation forms were established following patterns from spirits associated with religions that promote yoga.

Each religion originated from a spiritual entity providing clear instructions on achieving the state from which it came. For example, Buddhism is based on Buddha's reported visitation by a spirit showing him spiritual possibilities and how to attain them. A Christian practicing yoga in the manner Buddhism prescribes would have to be prepared to connect with the same spirit encountered by Buddha. This pattern is consistent across all non-Christian meditative practices.

Hypnosis

Hypnosis, another form of meditation, often involves a dynamic resembling that of a master and servant. The hypnotist, already in the state they aim to induce in someone else, must obtain consent from the individual they wish to hypnotize. Once in a trance-like state, the person loses control and is entirely under another's influence. While this might initially seem entertaining, the potential for harm is significant. Indeed, the experience of being demonically possessed is akin to being in a trance-like state.

New Age Techniques

Other non-Christian meditation forms emphasize the creative aspect of meditation. Manifestation, channelling, and other similar New Age techniques prioritize developing the ability to declare things that do not exist as though they did and to transform them into realities that are not currently manifest. For Christians, these practices might not immediately raise concerns because the outcomes of manifestation or the entities being channelled appear harmless. However, it's important to remember that not all that seems good comes from God.

The primary issue with these practices is their disregard for the will of God and genuine love for others, focusing instead on personal desires. The aims of manifestation or channelling can vary, from seeking the affection of those uninterested to coveting possessions or statuses one ought not to pursue. The devil is aware that this world operates on the principle of sowing and reaping. He has introduced variations of meditative practices based on this fundamental concept to lead many away from God's will. Any meditative practice that overlooks the will of God and genuine love for oneself and others cannot be from God and should be avoided.

Recognize the Risks

One reason many Christians are misled is their inability to recognize the risks of non-Christian meditation early on. If your current path is leading you toward danger, changing course before you find yourself in peril is prudent. For those in a precarious situation, akin to being in the lion's den, rescue is necessary. If you are experiencing demonic manifestations associated with practices like yoga, manifestation, channelling, and similar activities, you need deliverance. It's likely you have inadvertently allowed demonic spirits access to yourself. If this applies to you, repeat this prayer: "In the mighty name of Jesus Christ, I command every spirit that is not of God operating within me to depart now!" You are liberated in Jesus' name. Now, through the teachings of this book, you will learn the correct way to meditate.

CHRISTIAN MEDITATION

Meditation is akin to summoning a meeting. Who you allow in this meeting is based on your meditation approach. Whether you realize it or not, just like a person in a listening posture, a meditative person is signalling to spiritual forces that they are open to communication with them. Meditation is ideally a meeting geared towards positive outcomes. Negative outcomes can still be achieved when complaining, anxiety, fear, and worry are present while meditating.

In Christian meditation, a meeting is called between your entire self (spirit, soul, and body), the Spirit of God, and the Word of God. The evidence of a successful Christian meditation is when you come in agreement with the Holy Spirit and the Word of God. After meditating properly, your God-like status or God-consciousness would have increased. Remember, God said, *"Come and let us reason together [.]"* (Isaiah 1:18) You will never come out of a genuine meeting with God the same. Moses initially argued with God during his meeting in Exodus 3 but soon came in agreement and became a god unto Pharaoh. Hence, the version of Moses that went into the burning bush meeting with God was not the same version that came out. In the same vein, even Moses' staff was upgraded due to a time of meditation with God. While on earth, even Jesus Christ went into meetings with God through meditation and came out of it transformed and more empowered. Jesus' experience at the mountain of transfiguration resulted from meditation.

A Transportation System

Meditation is one of the most potent transportation systems for moving a person from one realm to another. When deeply and consistently done, meditation can not only take a person's mind and soul to another plane of existence but even the physical body can be moved. When Elijah was meditating with his head between his legs in 1 Kings 18:41-46, he was gathering the speed needed to operate in a superhuman state. His meditation gave him an advantage over time by speeding up his movement. Remember that it is written in scripture that we will reap what we sow (Galatians 6:7-9). This means we will reap more time when we intentionally sow time. Spending time is not equivalent to investing or sowing time, just as spending money differs from investing or giving it. The intentionality of using your time makes it a sowing exercise.

A Transformation System

Meditation is a system of transformation. In 2 Corinthians 3:18, the Bible tells us that we are transformed as we behold. In essence, we become what we behold. This is a deep spiritual principle. Our transformation is rooted in what we consistently and intentionally keep before us. Similar to how sleep enhances the body's ability to heal and grow, meditation enhances the body's, soul's, and spirit's transformation process. When a connection has been made with the spiritual realm, the flow of virtue moves from the more powerful to the less powerful.

Beholding Jesus

Our focus in meditation is to behold Jesus through His word, other expressions of Jesus, or any other revealed truth, and we will begin to transform into the same image. Many people typically do not know what happens to them during meditation because they only see the effect of meditation afterwards. Elijah did not start running faster than King Ahab's chariot while meditating but after meditation.

Fellowship with God

One of the most critical differences between Christian and non-Christian meditation is that Christian meditation practitioners seek fellowship with our heavenly Father through the Holy Spirit and the Word of God. It is essential to understand that meditation is simply a meeting, a transportation system from this realm into the spiritual realm, and a powerful divine transformation methodology. The result of your meditation could either be because you chose to enforce a strict guest list or perhaps allowed just about anyone to attend your "spiritual meeting." While in a typical meeting, we can confirm who is attending based on their physical or virtual identifiers, the nature of meditation means that we have to employ other means to confirm who is attempting to grace our meditative rendezvous. In subsequent chapters, I will share more details on assessing your meditation's success.

A Place of Agreement

Meditation is a place of potential agreement, where the Spirit of God, the Word of God, and the meditator come in agreement for creation, creativity, wisdom, restoration, transformation, and power to happen. 1 John 5:8 says, *"There are three that bear witness on earth: the Spirit, the water, and the blood; and these three agree as one."* The phrase "bear witness" can also mean "come in agreement" in meditation. Let's rephrase this scripture and say that three agree on the earth: the Spirit, the water, and the blood. The Spirit represents the Holy Spirit, the water represents the Word of God, and the blood represents the person. So then, if you have the Holy Spirit inside of you and the blood - which is yourself - then you already have a quorum for a powerful agreement.

The power of agreement is introduced in Matthew 18:18-20, where we are told that when at least two entities come to an agreement in making a request, God will not hold anything back from them. This means an agreement does not have to be between human beings alone. But more often than not, many of us are looking for agreement outside of ourselves when there is no agreement within us first. A house divided against itself cannot stand (Matthew 12:22-28). There cannot be agreement outside you. No wonder Jesus told him, *"If you can believe, all things are possible to him who believes."* (Mark 9:23) The more you meditate the right way, the easier it will be to have faith in God, yourself, and others.

BIBLICAL REFERENCES TO MEDITATION

Meditation is as old as the Bible itself. It is erroneous to believe that Christians who meditate are borrowing that practice from other religions.

From the book of Genesis, all the way to the book of Revelation, the art of meditation is clearly spoken about. The Bible both directly and indirectly mentions meditation. Genesis 24:63 shows that *"Isaac went out to meditate in the field in the evening."* Given Isaac's close relationship with his father, Abraham, and Abraham's intimate relationship with God, it can be inferred that Abraham taught his son to meditate. In Revelation 1:9-10, we see that John *"was on the island that is called Patmos for the Word of God and for the testimony of Jesus Christ."* John was also *"in the Spirit on the Lord's Day."* This means that John's focus in meditation while on the Island of Patmos was the Word of God and testimonies of Jesus Christ.

Here are some examples of scriptures that speak about meditation. The scriptures below are divided into three sections based on the three key stages of meditation: **Quietness, Visualization** and **Declaration.**

Quietness

- *"For thus says the Lord God, the Holy One of Israel: "In returning and rest you shall be saved; In quietness and confidence shall be your strength." But you would not [.]"* (Isaiah 30:15)

- *"Because he knows no quietness in his heart, He will not save anything he desires."* (Job 20:20)

- *"It stood still, But I could not discern its appearance. A form was before my eyes; There was silence; Then I heard a voice saying [.]"* (Job 4:16)

- *"A time to tear, And a time to sew; A time to keep silence, And a time to speak [.]"* (Ecclesiastes 3:7)

- *"Keep silence before Me, O coastlands, And let the people renew their strength! Let them come near, then let them speak; Let us come near together for judgment."* (Isaiah 41:1)

- *"But the Lord is in His holy temple. Let all the earth keep silence before Him."* (Habakkuk 2:20)

- *"Be silent in the presence of the Lord God; For the day of the Lord is at hand, For the Lord has prepared a sacrifice; He has invited His guests."* (Zephaniah 1:7)

- *"Oh, that you would be silent, And it would be your wisdom [.]"* (Job 13:5)

- *"Now the sons of the prophets who were at Bethel came out to Elisha, and said to him, "Do you know that the Lord will take away your master from over you today?" And he said, "Yes, I know; keep silent!"* (2 Kings 2:3)

- *"Now the sons of the prophets who were at Jericho came to Elisha and said to him, "Do you know that the Lord will take away your master from over you today?" So he answered, "Yes, I know; keep silent!"* (2 Kings 2:5)

- *"Truly my soul silently waits for God; From Him comes my salvation."* (Psalms 62:1)

- *"My soul, wait silently for God alone, For my expectation is from Him."* (Psalms 62:5)

- *"He was oppressed and He was afflicted, Yet He opened not His mouth; He was led as a lamb to the slaughter, And as a sheep before its shearers is silent, So He opened not His mouth."* (Isaiah 53:7)

- *"Set your mind on things above, not on things on the earth."* (Colossians 3:2)

Visualization

- *"But we all, with unveiled face, beholding as in a mirror the glory of the Lord, are being transformed into the same image from glory to glory, just as by the Spirit of the Lord."* (2 Corinthians 3:18)

- *Open my eyes, that I may see Wondrous things from Your law."* (Psalms 119:18)

- *"See, I have this day set you over the nations and over the kingdoms, To root out and to pull down, To destroy and to throw down, To build and to plant."* (Jeremiah 1:10)

- *"So the Lord said to Moses: "See, I have made you as God to Pharaoh, and Aaron your brother shall be your prophet.""* (Exodus 7:1)

- *"Finally, brethren, whatever things are true, whatever things are noble, whatever things are just, whatever things are pure, whatever things are lovely, whatever things are of good report, if there is any virtue and if there is anything praiseworthy—meditate on these things."* (Philippians 4:8)

- *"Set your mind on things above, not on things on the earth."* (Colossians 3:2)

- *"Again, the devil took Him up on an exceedingly high mountain, and showed Him all the kingdoms of the world and their glory."* (Matthew 4:8)

- *"I will meditate on the glorious splendor of Your majesty, And on Your wondrous works."* (Psalms 145:5)

- *"Let the words of my mouth and the meditation of my heart be acceptable in Your sight, O Lord, my strength and my Redeemer."* (Psalms 19:14)

- *"My mouth shall speak wisdom, And the meditation of my heart shall give understanding."* (Psalms 49:3)

- *"May my meditation be sweet to Him; I will be glad in the Lord."* (Psalms 104:34)

- *"Oh, how I love Your law! It is my meditation all the day."* (Psalms 119:97)

- *"I have more understanding than all my teachers, For Your testimonies are my meditation."* (Psalms 119:99)

- *"I call to remembrance my song in the night: I commune with mine own heart: and my spirit made diligent search."* (Psalms 77:6)

- *"Mine eyes prevent the night watches, that I might meditate in thy word."* (Psalms 119:148)

Declaration

- *"This Book of the Law shall not depart from your mouth, but you shall meditate in it day and night, that you may observe to do according to all that is written in it. For then you will make your way prosperous, and then you will have good success."* (Joshua 1:8)

- *But what does it say? "The word is near you, in your mouth and in your heart" (that is, the word of faith which we preach): that if you confess with your mouth the Lord Jesus and believe in your heart that God has raised Him from the dead, you will be saved. For with the heart one believes unto righteousness, and with the mouth, confession is made unto salvation. For the scripture says, "Whoever believes on Him will not be put to shame.* (Romans 10:8-11)

- *"Give ear to my words, O Lord, Consider my meditation."* (Psalms 5:1)

- *"A Meditation of David, which he sang to the Lord concerning the words of Cush, a Benjamite. O Lord my God, in You I put my trust; Save me from all those who persecute me; And deliver me."* (Psalms 7:1)

- *"Hear my voice, O God, in my meditation; Preserve my life from fear of the enemy."* (Psalms 64:1)

2

Benefits of Meditation

GENERATING THE POWER OF FAITH

Meditation is a way to generate the power of faith. Faith is one of the most powerful forces on the earth. Jesus said, "*With faith nothing shall be impossible for you.*" (Matthew 17:20) This means that the greater your faith, the greater your results. Can you imagine that Jesus visited a locality and could do no mighty work there because of their unbelief? (Mark 6:1-6) Imagine that there was a practice you could engage in regularly that would help to build your faith, which would then exponentially increase your success, would you diligently engage in it? This practice is meditation. There is no organization where meetings are not held as part of its daily activities. As explained earlier, meditation is like a meeting that has been called. When you meet with the right people, you will leave with a shift in mentality in the right direction. This positive shift in mentality is called faith. When you talk to God often, you will believe in Him. When you talk to the devil often, you will have doubts, fear, and worry.

The moment you catch the understanding of the use of meditation to grow your faith, you will never have issues with building your faith. Many of our issues with building faith stem from not having an understanding of what to do with our inner life. The conversations that matter are the ones that happen within us. This is why some rich countries rank lower on the happiness index while some poor nations rank surprisingly high on the same ranking. If you allow worry and negative thoughts to drown your thought life, you will be building "negative faith," which will lead to unbelief, fear, and other disastrous negative consequences.

Seeing is Believing

The beauty of meditation lies in its diversity. We can meditate on different things to bring us to the same destination. For instance, meditation can bring us to a place where we can visually see an outcome that we were once unable to see. Having now seen it, faith has risen. However, meditation on who God is and what He has done before can also have the same effect. It puts us in a state of "if He has done it before, He can do it again"; "If He has been good to me yesterday, He can be good to me today"; "If He did it for my father or my mother, would He not do it for me?" As you meditate along these lines, faith will begin to rise within you.

I approach every week with a positive mindset and declare, "This is the best week of my life." Why, you may ask? Because *"the path of the just is like the shining sun."* (Proverbs 4:18) We don't go down in the Kingdom; we go up! It might look like you are going down because you are going through a storm or a challenging time, similar to Christ on the cross, but *"having disarmed principalities and powers, He made a public spectacle of them, triumphing over them in it."* (Colossians 2:15) They thought Jesus was going down because He was on the cross. He must have been laughing on the inside, knowing that He would rise from the dead in three days.

Having faith is not the same as being optimistic or pessimistic. Having faith is not about ignoring the facts of a situation by burying your head in the sand and refusing to appraise the reality of a situation factually. Faith is about discovering God's thoughts on a situation and adopting that as your reality. This kind of conversation was seen in Ezekiel 37.

God's Report Vs. Our Report

In Ezekiel 37, the prophet Ezekiel was confronted with a dire situation. He found himself in a valley of bones. A valley is similar to a low point in life. A valley is a time of uncertainty, unpredictability, or perhaps even impending destruction or loss. The bones signify emptiness. The bones refer to loss and are a reminder of better yesteryears. The first thing God did was not give the prophet a pep talk about how all is well and that he should not worry, etc. Instead, God caused the prophet to accurately examine the situation and report back to Him. Prophet Ezekiel's response about the condition of the bones was, "*...behold, there were very many in the open valley; and indeed they were very dry.*" (Ezekiel 37:2) God is not shocked by the situation you are in. God is not moved by how dark your night might be or how dry your bones might be. God is the all-powerful, all-knowing, ever-present God.

In meditation, you take the situation to God through His Word or His Spirit and wait for heaven's report on that situation. Like the ambassador of a country will report a situation back to their home country, we are to allow God's Word and/or His Spirit to give us God's report on every situation. Faith, then, is holding onto God's report on every situation. Remember Isaiah 53:1, "*Who has believed our report? And to whom has the arm of the Lord been revealed.*" When we meditate, we exchange our earthly report for a heavenly assessment. Our faith increases as we adopt heaven's report concerning every area of our lives.

A practical example involves a person who just received a negative result. Instead of panicking and naturally leaning towards the worst-case scenario, call a meeting with Divinity through meditation. Find a quiet place where you can focus. Depending on the situation, you can even schedule time away from the hustle of life in a retreat. Alternatively, finding a time of day when you can be by yourself could suffice. Locate two or three scriptures that speak to God's will concerning your health. Perhaps you can find two or three anointed messages related to physical healing. Ensure that the messages are preached by preachers who have clear proof in the area of divine healing. During the time by yourself, think through the scriptures or the messages as you engage with them. Allow the questions you have concerning whether what you are reading or watching is true to bubble to the surface of your heart.

At the very same time, allow God to convince you that His will is for you. If you have ever witnessed a civil debate, you know that both parties are allowed to present their arguments until one side's argument overcomes that of the other. Some people might get to the point of agreement with God sooner than others. Your faith-building exercise in meditation concerning your divine healing is not over until you are convinced that God is right and the physical ailment or diagnosis is wrong. At this point, you are already healed and will just need to wait for the manifestation of that healing.

While in meditation, you can also be told how to eliminate the health issue. I want to stress that your faith-building through meditation is not over until you have exchanged your negative or incorrect thoughts with God's report concerning that situation. It is tough not to believe something you have seen and heard (1 John 1:1-3). Meditation will help you see, hear, and perceive what God wants you to see, hear, and perceive to build your faith.

PEACE

Peace is a heavenly virtue needed to flow in the supernatural realm. There are depths in the Spirit you will not know until your mind, body, and emotions are still in the presence of God. But be encouraged, my friend! Jesus, the Prince of Peace Himself, has given us the master key for generating the peace of God in all aspects of our being. John 14:27 tells us that Jesus does not give peace like the world does. If so, the question becomes, "How does Jesus give peace?" The peace that Christ has to offer comes through meditation.

Imagine someone going to a new seafood restaurant and ordering a meal that leaves their stomach wishing they had fasted that day. They are offered the same food at another time and take it. What word would best describe such a person? Or, imagine a situation where this same person receives news that makes their heart sink to their stomach and then goes on to replay the same news moments later. It is obvious that this individual lives a life devoid of lasting peace.

Christ's Peace is a Choice

It is a choice not to allow your heart to be troubled because of your confidence in the finished work of Christ on the cross. Jesus said, *"Come to Me, all you who labor and are heavy laden, and I will give you rest. Take My yoke upon you and learn from Me, for I am gentle and lowly in heart, and you will find rest for your souls. For My yoke is easy, and My burden is light."* (Matthew 11:28-30) Lasting peace comes from a lifestyle of grace, not works. Lasting peace comes from an understanding that, after all is said and done, you are who you are by the grace of God. Lasting peace is possible, but it involves a shift in mindset.

We see an admirable example in Christ's interaction with His disciples when He got news of Lazarus' sickness and eventual death (John 11:1-44). When the disciples came and told Jesus that Lazarus was dead, Jesus ensured that was the last time he heard that news. The first lesson to learn here is to *only receive bad news once.* After the first time Jesus was told about Lazarus' sickness and later death, Jesus spoke life and confessed what he desired to see, saying that Lazarus was sleeping. Jesus did not let His disciples' interpretation of Lazarus' state trouble His heart. Just as the scripture says, *"As a man thinks in his heart, so is he."* (Proverbs 23:7) Even though Jesus' disciples were still stuck on the fact that Lazarus was sick and eventually died, Jesus had already moved to the realm of believing Lazarus was only sleeping. Operating in the realm of peace is a function of your faith that everything will work together for your good because you love God and are called according to His purpose (Romans 8:28).

Embodying Peace

The peace of God is generated when you take scriptures on peace and meditate on them. Just as the scripture says, *"As a man thinks in his heart, so is he."* (Proverbs 23:7) Meditation will take you from the realm of thought to the realm of reality. As you reflect deeply on scriptures about peace, you will gradually embody peace. Friend, it is as practical as setting time aside every day to fix your gaze on the peace of God. An example of this can look like the following:

Day One: *"Peace I leave with you, My peace I give to you; not as the world gives do I give to you. Let not your heart be troubled, neither let it be afraid."* (John 14:27)

Day Two: *"Glory to God in the highest, and on earth peace, goodwill toward men!"* (Luke 2:14)

Day Three: *"And let the peace of God rule in your hearts, to which also you were called in one body; and be thankful."* (Colossians 3:15)

By day Seven, Ten, or even Twenty, you would have become an embodiment of peace!

The Mind is a Planting Ground

The mind is the planting ground for meditation, where the seeds needed are sown. Since it's the same mind that needs peace and it makes meditation more effective when properly done. If you neglect your planting ground, weeds will grow, which will erode your peace. It's crucial to understand that the process of planting seeds may take time before yielding fruitful results. Initially, you may experience some turbulence, but by persistently planting good fruit in your mind for forty consistent days, you'll achieve and benefit from a stable, lush, and fruitful mind.

The 40-Day Principle

The 40-day rule holds significant importance in the Kingdom of God, especially for addressing foundational issues. Moses spent 40 days with God on the mountain to receive laws that would reshape the foundations of Israeli society. Similarly, Jesus Christ also spent 40 days in the wilderness fasting and praying to prepare for the restoration of the foundations of righteousness.

A harmful application of the 40-day principle can be seen when a bully repeatedly uses negative words to harass someone. Initially, being called stupid may be laughable and frustrating, but it is relatively easier to reject or resist. However, if the bullying continues, the person may begin to accept and believe these derogatory statements. By the tenth day, the taunting becomes deeply ingrained and the person resolves to stop resisting them. By the twentieth day, unless God helps a person, they may even start calling themselves stupid. This illustrates how the enemy can manipulate something good to derail God's children, similar to how Goliath consistently bullied the Israelites when the Philistines gathered to wage war against the Israelites. We read in 1 Samuel 17:16, *"And the Philistine drew near and presented himself forty days, morning and evening."* Anything you hear consistently for this long is bound to be imprinted in your mind.

The conclusion is that peace can be generated through meditation. In meditation, we connect with Jesus Christ, the Prince of Peace (Isaiah 9:6). The peace derived from meditation is generated as we direct our thoughts and attention towards positive and rightful things while eschewing the negative. Philippians 4:6-8 succinctly encapsulates this principle, urging us to focus on what is true, noble, right, pure, lovely, and admirable, ensuring our meditation fosters peace:

Be anxious for nothing, but in everything by prayer and supplication, with thanksgiving, let your requests be made known to God; and the peace of God, which surpasses all understanding, will guard your hearts and minds through Christ Jesus. Finally, brethren, whatever things are true, whatever things are noble, whatever things are just, whatever things are pure, whatever things are lovely, whatever things are of good report, if there is any virtue and if there is anything praiseworthy—meditate on these things.

Declaration Over Anxiety

In Jesus' mighty name, I will not give in to anxiety from today on. I will give thanks to God daily for His goodness in my life. I will always keep the right thoughts in my mind and never give in to negative thoughts.

DIVINE WISDOM

Meditation helps you tap into the wisdom of God that has already been deposited in you. Meditation is a powerful transportation system for transmitting wisdom from your spirit to your soul, encompassing your mind, will, and emotions. There is a lot that your spirit carries that your mind has yet to catch up to. 1 Corinthians 2:11 says *"for who among men knows the thoughts of a man except the spirit of the man that is in him?"* This highlights that there are deep aspects of yourself that only your human spirit can unveil. Meditation acts as a tool to access these profound depths. It's comparable to having unopened letters in your mailbox; one might complain about not receiving information already mailed without being aware that it has already arrived and awaits in their mailbox.

Similarly, many seek external solutions to their challenges, when in fact they ought to look within to gain wisdom. If I asked a university graduate the first thing they learned in highschool, they might not be able to remember. If the individual did, that would be very strange! Yet, that information is deep within the individual's spirit because it is born of God and is filled with wisdom and knowledge.

Divine Direction and Guidance

Many years ago, as a youth pastor, I was playing soccer on a grass field during a church picnic. It did not occur to me at that time that I had a single key in my pocket. The game started, and I became so submerged in the game as if I were playing a Premiership match. At the end of the game, I made my way back into the church building to catch my breath. I then checked my pocket only to realize that my key was missing! One of the youths was walking past me and must have noticed I had a puzzled look on my face, so I told her that I had lost my key while playing soccer. This youth member responded, "Pastor, you taught us that when we do not know what to do, we can ask the Holy Spirit and He can help us." Thank God for wonderful people who pay attention during a message and have the mind of Christ! To tell you the truth, when she said this, I did not believe it at first; but, I didn't want to rob this youth of the faith she had. So, I decided to walk back to the field and thought to myself, "It is finished today. How will I come and tell this youth that the principle I taught did not work?"

On the one hand, I was searching for the key, but on the other hand, I frantically thought about how I would explain the outcome to the youth member without shattering her faith. However, I continued walking through the field, praying in the Spirit, not knowing how I was going to find this single key. Then, suddenly, I stopped where I was in my tracks, looked down, and saw something shiny! I picked up what was shining in the sun, and lo and behold, it was my missing key! Mighty God, did I feel relief! I felt like Rhoda, the slave, when she went to open the door for Peter. Rhoda saw Peter and quickly shut the door on him in shock as she ran back to share the good news of Peter's arrival. I quickly grabbed the key and charged back to the church like a champion!

My spirit knew when the key fell out of my pocket, but I didn't realize it because I was focused on playing soccer. The Bible says that through meditation, we can connect our mind to our own spirit, *"The spirit of a man is the lamp of the Lord, searching all the inner depths of his heart."* (Proverbs 20:27) Even those who don't believe in the Holy Spirit meditate and gain wisdom as a result. According to Proverbs 20:27, God uses our spirit as a lamp to search the depths of our heart. The Lord uses a lamp, "spirit," to search the heart because the lamp brings to the surface and uncovers what is either hidden or missing.

Friend, if you know how to use your spirit, you can locate any hidden or missing information. If I said to you, "Do you see that over there?" and pointed in a particular direction, you would turn your physical eyes to where I am pointing. While we have learned how to engage our physical bodies in navigating the physical world, we must also learn how to use our spirit in navigating the unseen realm. In the same way, the spirit of a man can be learned and taught how to take direction to locate information. Meditation can take you to realms you've never been to before.

Persisting in Meditation

Staying the course in the place of meditation is the key to drawing wisdom while meditating. David said, *"Yea, though I walk through the valley of the shadow of death, I will fear no evil [.]"* (Psalms 23:4) Yes, he wasn't speaking of an imagined valley of death, but of a real death experience, yet he stayed the course. The realm of meditation is a place where one can experience both manifestations of life and death. In either experience, the goal is to stay the course and keep your mind focused on Christ in meditation. Meditation exposes a person to the reality of both darkness and light. Many people stop meditating when it seems like they are traversing the valley of the shadow of death. While death can be understood as a form of darkness, it is not to be feared but explored. God Himself promises to give us treasures that can only be found in darkness (Isaiah 45:3).

Wisdom is Hidden in Darkness

Wisdom is one of the treasures that can be found in darkness. Choosing to remain in the place of meditation, despite your initial unpleasant experience, will place you en route to accessing depths of wisdom in the Spirit. The turbulence you experience at the onset of meditation can be likened to when a plane is taking off. At the start, there is a lot of movement that can cause those in the plane to feel afraid. However, after it has taken off, it will eventually reach a comfortable altitude. In meditation, your response to darkness or fear will determine whether you will transcend to a higher realm and be given access to the hidden treasures in secret places.

ACCESS TO INFORMATION

God said to Jeremiah, *"Call to Me, and I will answer you, and show you great and mighty things, which you do not know."* (Jeremiah 33:3) God is omniscient, which means that He knows absolutely everything. He knows everything about the past, the present, and the future. Meditating the right way will enable you to connect with God for information. There is wisdom that comes from the spirit of man, demonic spirits, and there is the divine wisdom that comes from the Spirit of God. In search of information, many people seek palm readers and diviners not knowing that they are playing with fire. Most times, these spiritualists manipulate people into exposing themselves to demonic forces. They have learned how to communicate with demonic entities. Such people can scan different parts of your body to connect with your spirit; from there, they can gain information from your spirit that you didn't even know you had.

Demonic Sources of Information

Palm readers and diviners are fraudulent spiritualists. They only have access to information they are given. In some ways, they are similar to medical practitioners, in that when given information about a patient's condition, they conduct tests to produce a medical explanation. Medical practitioners, however, practice within legal and ethical boundaries with the purpose of bringing solutions to the health challenges within society. Diviners, on the other hand, practice with the sole purpose to exploit, manipulate, deceive, and destroy vulnerable people. They deceive them into sharing details of their life, which gives them access to more information about a person's past, present, and future. This is one of the devil's tools for gathering information about people. The devil does not know the future. The information the devil gets is found in people.

Divine Sources of Information

Every time we come into the presence of God, there is an outpouring of divine information into our spirit in the form of light. Your mind may not always recognize when this deposit is taking place, but your spirit keeps a record of every word and impartation. Due to this lack of spiritual awareness, the enemy often waits to attack a child of God after they have been powerfully imparted in a service or through association with an anointed vessel. The enemy's mission and vision have never changed; it has always been and will continue to be, to kill, steal, and destroy (John 10:10).

We can connect with the Spirit of God through meditation to gain access to information for solutions. I have received solutions from God that I didn't know were solutions until five years later. Many times, I discovered I had the solution in the midst of a challenge. Meditation takes you to the realm of searching for information. What you search out through meditation will be found. You cannot continually meditate on having a divorce and expect to enjoy information that will lead to a blissful marriage. You cannot think you are a grasshopper and expect to receive information to help you trample over your enemy. Make up your mind to start meditating based on the word of God today so you can gain access to divine revelation.

Hearing God's Voice in Darkness

Always remember that the voice of God is loudest in darkness. The darkness in this scripture below is not demonic darkness. It is simply the lack of light that occurs at nighttime. When properly done, meditation simulates the darkness that is needed to hear God loudly.

"These words the Lord spoke to all your assembly, in the mountain from the midst of the fire, the cloud, and the thick darkness, with a loud voice; and He added no more. And He wrote them on two tablets of stone and gave them to me." (Deuteronomy 5:22)

Meditation first takes us to a place of quietness before we get to the place of hearing God. One of the prophetic codes is the prophet's use of the nighttime and darkness in accessing the voice of God. In the scripture below, God was passing judgment on the prophets and saying that the strategy that has always worked in helping them access God's voice was not going to work anymore because they were in sin.

"Therefore you shall have night without vision, and you shall have darkness without divination; The sun shall go down on the prophets, and the day shall be dark for them." (Micah 3:6)

INTIMACY WITH GOD

One of the benefits that meditation offers is intimacy with God. Our lives are increasingly getting busier and busier. The technological advancement we were promised would improve lives has, to a large extent, negatively impacted relationships. Technology and other social platforms have eaten deep into our ability to focus. The most important relationship a child of God should maintain is their relationship with Jesus. Since it is practically impossible to develop intimacy with an important personality like God without focus, except drastic steps are taken, it will be difficult for the next generation of believers to develop intimacy with Jesus. One of the solutions the Lord has made available is meditation. In Jeremiah 29:13, God said, *"And you will seek Me and find Me when you search for Me with all your heart."* Meditation helps us to search for God with all our heart, moments at a time until it becomes the norm.

Spend Focused Time with God

It is known that what we do consistently will quickly become a habit and run subconsciously. As you develop the habit of spending focused time in God's Word in meditation, you will soon realize that your mind will get more focused on God. Have you ever felt that you were far away from God? We have all felt that at some point in our walk with God. The solution is meditation. What makes retreats a very powerful experience is the fact that we are able to focus our attention on Christ. However, it is not realistic to always leave our assignment to go on retreats. Meditation will make your lives seem like you are perpetually in a retreat. Our decision to meditate is us saying to God, "I am willing to seek You with all my heart." God has promised you will find Him when you seek Him with all your heart. All you have to do is make a decision to set aside time to meditate based on what you will learn from the pages of this book. You will return with testimonies of deeper intimacy with Jesus as a result, in Jesus' name.

Pay Attention to Christ's Prompting

One powerful scripture that assures us of deeper intimacy with Christ through meditation is Revelation 3:20. Jesus said, *"Behold, I stand at the door and knock. If anyone hears My voice and opens the door, I will come in to him and dine with him, and he with Me."* Meditation will help you to see Jesus at the door of your heart, hear Him knock on your heart, and hear His voice, which will lead to deeper intimacy and fellowship with Him. A consistent cycle of living a distracted life will lead to us missing the "knocks" from Christ for fellowship. Remember, *"For where your treasure is, there your heart will be also."* (Matthew 6:21)

Technological advancement has come with a strong ability to capture our minds, will, and emotions in ways we have not seen. For you to enjoy the best of life and still have your heart reserved for Christ, you will have to make a decision to apply self-control while navigating the technological landscape. Are you ready to open the door of your heart by meditating on God's Word and His nature? Continue reading as I show you how to make the best of the art of meditation.

Healing and Deliverance

Everything available in Christ becomes accessible when Christ shows up. If meditation brings you into an experience with Christ, it means that all the treasures in Christ are at your disposal. You have to understand that the moment light appears, darkness must disappear. The Bible tells us that Jesus came to destroy the works of the devil (1 John 3:8). Jesus was anointed by God with the Holy Spirit to do good and heal all who were oppressed by the devil, for God was with Him (Acts 10:38). People who have joined our Hour of Meditation (HoM) have been surprised at the rate of miracles just by following the guided meditation sessions I run.

The Power of Agreement

It might look simple, but the principles at work are biblically sound and spiritually profound. Once there is agreement, divinity has the right to manifest in humanity. No creation can occur without a quorum of agreement. Right from the beginning of creation, God showed the place of agreement in creation. God cannot be summoned, or a god (mankind) created without agreement. So God said, *"Let Us make man in Our own image, according to Our likeness..."* (Genesis 1:26) Likewise, we were told in Matthew 18:19-20 that *"...if two of you agree on earth concerning anything that they ask, it will be done for them by My Father in heaven. For where two or three are gathered together in My name, I am there in the midst of them."* The greatest miracles are done effortlessly when Jesus is invited and permitted to operate freely in the midst of the people. The more people who come in agreement to invite Christ, the greater the power He will display when He shows up. It's the power of agreement.

The woman with the issue of blood for twelve years came in agreement with herself to touch the hem of Christ's garment (Luke 8:43-48). It is one thing for Christ to show up in your midst and another to choose to touch Him or allow Him to touch you. Apostle Peter introduced us to a new dimension in the appearance of the risen Christ when he said to a diseased man, *"Aeneas, Jesus the Christ heals you. Arise and make your bed."* (Acts 9:34) Even though Peter was the one standing in front of the man, Peter said it was Jesus Christ who was healing him.

Recognizing Christ's Manifestations

Are you able to identify Christ when He shows up in your midst? Meditation will allow us to capture the aura of heaven so we can identify Christ or any heavenly personality, however they choose to manifest themselves. Just like it would be hard to explain what my mother's voice sounds like, it is hard to explain what experiencing God looks like. The best way to know Christ is to fellowship with Him through meditation. The more you know Him, the more you will love Him and invite Him to take over every aspect of your life.

Alignment

I have shared many benefits of meditation, but alignment is one of the most powerful. What does it mean to be aligned? Alignment means to walk with God. Jesus told His new disciples, *"Follow Me, and I will make you fishers of men."* (Matthew 4:19) In essence, as they followed Christ, they would find themselves operating productively in life. John 5 shows us that alignment with the Father was one of Jesus' important missions on earth. Meditation enables us to walk in step with divinity. Anxiety, worry, fear, covetousness, and other anomalies either cause a person to go ahead of God or walk behind Him. Constant meditation will lead a person to a place of equilibrium and equipoise regularly. When you come to this point, 2 Kings 3:17 will become a reality for you:

"For *thus says the Lord: 'You shall not see wind, nor shall you see rain; yet that valley shall be filled with water, so that you, your cattle, and your animals may drink.'"*

Living a Supernatural Life

Walking in alignment with God will make every day of your life supernatural, even though it might not always be spectacular. It is often said that we should not live our lives based on miracles. In meditation, we come to reason with God. Do you know that you tend to walk in alignment with someone you are talking to while walking? The moon walks in alignment with the sun daily, hence its ability to shine. I pray that as you meditate regularly, you will come into alignment with the King of kings and Lord of lords.

3

Christian Meditation Approaches

I mentioned earlier in this book that meditation can be understood based on the principle of farming. At a fundamental level, farming involves clearing the ground, planting seeds, and harvesting what was planted. Similarly, the three stages of meditation are **Quietness, Visualization**, and **Declaration**.

Quietness prepares your heart for meditation by eliminating worry, anxiety, and anything else hampering your focus. The visualization stage is where we plant the Word of God in our hearts. The declaration stage is the process of harvesting the crops that came from the visualization stage.

QUIETNESS

Have you wondered why the Lord clarified that we should meditate on certain things while avoiding others? It is because the heart God created us with can produce after its kind. As a man thinks, so is he (Proverbs 23:7). In Philippians 4:8, we are told to only meditate on *"whatever things are true, whatever things are noble, whatever things are just, whatever things are pure, whatever things are lovely, whatever things are of good report, if there is any virtue and if there is anything praiseworthy..."* This admonishment is because a heart not focused on thoughts of this nature will not be a good ground for visualization. The goal of quietness is not necessarily to have an empty mind but to be realigned to a thought life that is based on Philippians 4:8 and the peace referred to in Philippians 4:7, *"and the peace of God, which surpasses all understanding, will guard your hearts and minds through Christ Jesus, restored to your heart.* A heart that is not at peace cannot host the presence of God.

The Importance of Quietness In Meditation

It Yields Rest and Confidence

Isaiah 30:15 helps us see that the end result of quietness is rest and confidence. In this meditation phase, we are regulating ourselves to get back to a place of rest and confidence regardless of what is happening in and around us. If God Himself gave that prescription, we must take it seriously. There are many things happening in our world or the world at large that can upset our peace. We have to utilize the quietness segment of meditation to remind ourselves of the truth so we can be realigned and regulated. The time of quietness is a time to remind ourselves of what really matters. Quietness will help to untangle us from the mental and emotional webs we have allowed to exist in our hearts and minds. Do you remember how many cultures soothe a crying child? The adult pretty much carries the child (if possible) and rocks the child back and forth while also singing or saying nice words to the child. We should do something similar to ourselves when we are trying to bring ourselves to a place of quietness.

Quietness Is An Instruction From God

Silence or quietness is also an instruction from God for us to stop speaking so we can communicate with Him. Ecclesiastes 3:7 makes it clearer in advising that there is *"A time to keep silence, And a time to speak [.]"* Our interaction with divinity must be with the understanding that we are talking to the King of glory. While we must be confident enough to share our opinions and speak to God, we also have to note that there must be honour and respect as we approach God's throne. In (Isaiah 41:1), God gave clear instructions to *"Keep silence before Me, O coastlands, And let the people renew their strength! Let them come near, then let them speak; Let us come near together for judgment."* This, in essence, is the same as Solomon saying, *"there is time for everything."* There are times that we talk ourselves into a frenzy, and we need to know when to just be quiet. The prophet Habakkuk clearly advises that *"...the Lord is in His holy temple. Let all the earth keep silence before Him."* (Habakkuk 2:20)

Job 13:5 says the same thing but in a different way, *"Oh, that you would be silent, And it would be your wisdom!"* Are you ready to receive wisdom from the Lord? Then we have to come to Him in quietness and confidence.

Overcoming Negative Thoughts

As you have now seen, quietness can be about keeping silent, and sometimes, it also involves speaking over negative thoughts. If you are already having the right thoughts, the quietness you need might be silence. If you are struggling with anxiety, worry, etc., the quietness you need is to impose the right thoughts through your words. As you see me do at the Hour of Meditation, begin quietness by reminding yourself of what is true. Imagine yourself trying to calm down a friend who is feeling troubled. What would you say to such a person? I am sure that you would say, "Don't worry, all will be well". Perhaps you will also remind them of who God is and why, regardless of what happens, they will come out on top and victorious. I have noticed that people are able to say to others what they are unable to say to themselves. It is easy for a person to tell someone else that everything will be well and not believe it if they say the same thing to themselves.

Quietness in Scripture

Jesus

Have you wondered how Jesus made it through the crucifixion? He was in a meditative state. Remember that Jesus faced the cross, as we are all expected to face challenges with the empowerment of the Holy Spirit. It means that we could also go through the same experience as He did with the help of the Holy Spirit. Prophet Isaiah gave us more context when he shared that Jesus, "*Was oppressed and He was afflicted, yet He opened not His mouth; He was led as a lamb to the slaughter, and as a sheep before its shearers is silent, So He opened not His mouth.*" (Isaiah 53:7) As a side note, talking is one of the ways that energy leaks. The time of battle on the cross was not a time to argue, worry, gossip, etc. May the Lord grant you the grace to discern when to speak and when to be quiet in Jesus' name.

David

One man who walked with God and received glowing praise from God was David. In fact, God called David a man after His own heart (1 Samuel 13:14). David said, "*Truly my soul silently waits for God; from Him comes my salvation.*" (Psalms 62:1) David also stated, "*My soul, wait silently for*

God alone, for my expectation is from Him." (Psalms 62:5) David also spoke about another method for quietness, which is to superimpose unhealthy thoughts with the right thoughts. According to David, we will not struggle much with unhealthy thoughts if we are able to maintain quietness throughout the day by meditating on the right thoughts.

- *"Oh, how I love Your law! It is my meditation all the day."* (Psalms 119:97)

- *"I have more understanding than all my teachers, For Your testimonies are my meditation."* (Psalms 119:99)

- *"I call to remember my song in the night: I meditate with my own heart: and my spirit made diligent search."* (Psalms 77:6)

- *"Mine eyes prevent the night watches, that I might meditate in thy word."* (Psalms 119:148)

VISUALIZATION

Visualization is a key aspect of meditation; it serves as the engine. It involves the use of images and experiences to aid your meditation. Visualization is the aspect of meditation that involves planting the seeds of the Word of God into your heart. The Word is like a cheque we have received. It must be deposited into our hearts. The Word can dislodge whatever is hindering us from moving forward. Visualization is about generating a picture of your life based on what the Word of God says. You can remove the name in any scripture you desire and put yours instead; it is allowed. Once God has said something, it carries immense power that cannot be denied. It is known that even demonic practitioners utilize prophetic books in the Bible because of their potency.

Determining What You Visualize

Start with Your Areas of Challenges

If you're naturally weak, begin to visualize strength. Find three scriptures on strength in the Bible and begin to visualize yourself in them. For example, "*The joy of the Lord is my strength.*" (Nehemiah 8:10) Do not move away from meditating on the scripture until you have gained the strength.

Perhaps poverty is the next problem. Locate scriptures that speak to supernatural wealth and meditate on them. For example, "*My God shall supply all my needs according to His riches in Christ Jesus.*" (Philippians 4:19)

Visualize in Alignment with God's Will

Let your environment, pictures, words, etc., enhance your visualization in the direction of whatever word the Lord has spoken over you. Visualization should not involve imposing your own cravings, desires, and thoughts upon God. Filling your mind with your own cravings, desires, and thoughts during visualization without leaving space for the will of God can lead you down a misguided and dangerous path. This is why the will of God, as stated in His Word and through revelations to you, *must* consistently form the foundation of your visualization.

Explore Scriptures as You Meditate

While visualizing, we examine the implication of what God has said to our past, present, and future. Not all scriptures carry the same power when it comes to visualization. Jesus said, "...*The words that I speak to you are spirit, and they are life.*" (John 6:63) While it is true that the Bible is the Word of God, not every word spoken in the Bible is true. The Bible documents words spoken by the devil, demons, as well as weak and wicked people. Hence, while searching for words to use in visualization, know that the personality of the person who spoke those words matters. What Jesus said, for example, will carry more spiritual weight than words spoken by other people or demonic personalities.

Let's assume I want to visualize Isaiah 11:5-9 while in meditation.

Righteousness shall be the belt of His loins, And faithfulness the belt of His waist. "The wolf also shall dwell with the lamb, The leopard shall lie down with the young goat, The calf and the young lion and the fatling together; And a little child shall lead them. The cow and the bear shall graze; Their young ones shall lie down together; And the lion shall eat straw like the ox. The nursing child shall play by the cobra's hole, And the weaned child shall put his hand in the viper's den. They shall not hurt nor destroy in all My holy mountain, For the earth shall be full of the knowledge of the Lord As the waters cover the sea."

Remember that meditation is like a meeting between the Holy Spirit, the Word and you. Let's go through this scripture and ask ourselves pertinent questions: *Where is the holy mountain? Who is the mountain? Is it after I die, or is it on the earth?* Maybe the Lord would respond with a follow-up question: *Was the Garden of Eden in heaven or here on the earth?* Such a question is loaded and can be pondered on for days, weeks, or even months.

Your exploration of this study in the Word can take you to scriptures that speak about the Garden of Eden. The Bible talked about the rivers of Pishon, Gihon, and all those places. It was a place on the earth, but the moment God chased Adam and Eve from the Garden of Eden, it was elevated into a spiritual plane.

When many of us have visitations, and we have dreams and certain encounters where we go to certain places, we give it the generic name of heaven. It is not only heaven that we can visit. Heaven is not the only realm. It is in the same way we call every spirit an angel. You see that it is not human, so you call it an angel, but there are distinctions.

When Jesus spoke in Mark 4, He spoke to the wind and the sea, and they heard the specific things He said. In like manner, there are words for your kidneys, your liver, your eyes, and every part of your being. When you meditate and visualize, don't give yourself the answers to your musings; instead, receive the answers from the Holy Spirit through the Word.

For example, in Matthew 5:14, Jesus says we are a city set on a hill that cannot be hidden. As you begin meditating on it, this scripture will take you to another scripture, and then another scripture, and then by the time you are done, you might have triangulated six scriptures which then solidify this truth. By the time you step out from your visualization and someone in your home screams because something bad happened, you will not panic because you know that your house is a holy mountain. I read a testimony in a book about how a lady encountered a snake in her home. She froze immediately when she saw it. The snake was coming towards her to strike, but it kept hitting something in front of her that was invisible, like glass. It kept hitting this barrier until it disintegrated and disappeared.

Utilizing Other Channels of Grace

When you are praying in the Spirit, praying in your understanding, worshiping, or reading the Word, your mind can distract you from focus and concentration. One way to utilize visualization when praying in the Spirit is to focus your mind on what is coming out of your mouth. This focus will help you receive the life in the words as you focus on them. Attempt to "see" the words coming out of your mouth until you are no longer aware of your environment. At this point, you will have entered a deeply meditative state.

Creating Through Visualization

As you regularly visualize in meditation, you will be excited when you see problems because solutions would have already come from your place of meditation. People who solve problems are those with an active inner life based on the Word. Consider this; if the world we live in is created by our visualization, whose visualization has created your own world? Great thinkers have always been accused of either heresy, losing their minds, being unrealistic, etc. However, the reality is that trailblazers, pathfinders, and trendsetters visualize outside the box. They typically visualize what can be instead of what was or what is. They visualize in realms that regular people might be afraid of delving into. Nobody is going to arrest you for visualizing your ideal future based on the Word. Don't be afraid to visualize outside the norm. If the Word of God is your seed for meditation, you can safely visualize without the risk of losing your mind or a sense of reality.

This principle of visualization does not only work for humans. It also works on animals. Jacob was instructed to make animals visualize the nature of offspring he wanted them to give birth to, and that is what they gave birth to (Genesis 30:37-43). The spiritual law is that we reproduce after our visualization, not after our kind. The flocks that Jacob made to visualize had no other option but to produce offspring according to what they looked at while mating.

Many years ago, while I was praying, the Holy Spirit answered a question I had in my heart about raising children. I always wondered why it was generally believed that pastors' children did not turn out well. That day while praying, the Holy Spirit told me that many pastors' children do not turn out well because the pastors do not allow their children to be in close enough proximity to visualize them. Some of them are so busy that the children end up visualizing someone else who is in close proximity to the children. So, we do not naturally reproduce after our kind. We reproduce based on who or what we visualize. This principle can be intentionally applied to enable you to succeed in any field of endeavour.

Check Your Heart Posture

To fully benefit from meditation, we are encouraged to approach God with an unveiled face (2 Corinthians 3:18). Upon becoming born again and embarking on meditation, one role of the Holy Spirit, with our consent, is to purify our hearts of ungodly desires, passions, cravings, and more. The state of our heart might delay the manifestation of a believer's desires from the Lord. This state refers to the extent to which our desires align with those of the Lord. An unveiled face also signifies approaching the Lord with authenticity.

Consider this; can you conceal something physical when passing through an X-ray machine? In meditation, we must permit the Spirit of the Lord to examine us and assess various facets of our lives. The unrestricted access to our hearts that we grant the Lord will determine the magnitude to which He can shape us into His likeness. Beyond the fulfillment of any specific desires, perhaps the most transformative outcome of meditation is our potential to become like God.

Visualization in Scripture

Abraham

God appeared to Abraham and taught him how to meditate, specifically how to visualize. This is why Abraham is the father of faith. He was given the machinery for meditation that enabled him to produce faith again and again. God personally coached Abraham on how to visualize. In essence, the Lord taught Abraham to locate similitudes of what we desire from God and use that to sustain a picture of our expectations.

Secondly, God showed Abraham the process of deepening the impact of the encounters just by building altars to memorialize the encounter. Many of us have had visionary encounters that did not extend too far in determining the course of events because we didn't use it as a seed for visualization. The next time God visited Abraham, do you think Abraham needed to be told to identify something he could use to further the vision he received? I don't think so.

After these things the word of the Lord came to Abram in a vision, saying, "Do not be afraid, Abram. I am your shield, your exceedingly great reward." But Abram said, "Lord God, what will You give me, seeing I go childless, and the heir of my house is Eliezer of Damascus?" Then Abram said, "Look, You have given me no offspring; indeed one born in my house is my heir!" And behold, the word of the Lord came to him, saying, "This one shall not be your heir, but one who will come from your own body shall be your heir." Then He brought him outside and said, "Look now toward heaven, and count the stars if you are able to number them." And He said to him, "So shall your descendants be."And he believed in the Lord, and He accounted it to him for righteousness. (Genesis 15:1-6)

Declaration

Having calmed your thoughts and found a place of mental peace, as well as visualizing your desires according to the Word of God, the subsequent step is to enforce your harvest. Analogous to a woman who, despite undergoing her reproductive cycle and ovulating, will not conceive without engaging in sexual intercourse, our visualizations will only remain fantasies until we make declarations of faith. These declarations transition our visualizations from the spiritual realm into our earthly realm.

In teaching His disciples about faith and prayer, Jesus stated, *"whatever things you ask when you pray, believe that you receive them, and you will have them."* (Mark 11:24) This underscores the necessity of visualizing our prayer requests with the anticipation of their fulfillment. Visualization offers us a chance to "try out" or "window shop" our desires, determining if they align with our true aspirations. The act of declaration is then akin to "making payment" for our desires, claiming them as our own.

Each phase of meditation is interconnected, and each spiritual practice ordained by God serves a distinctive purpose. Bypassing the visualization aspect of meditation and immediately making declarations is one reason many fail to see their declarations manifest. Conversely, solely visualizing without making declarations results in frustration from the lack of materialized desires. This discrepancy has led many believers to develop cynicism, having read about the possibilities in scripture and heard testimonies of God's workings in others' lives without witnessing similar outcomes on their own. Can one be nourished by merely chewing food without swallowing it?

The Power of Your Declarations

Do not be misled by the notion that your words are devoid of significance and power. A farmer who has planted his seed cannot be convinced that his effort is futile. Your words possess power, but you must vocalize them for this power to materialize in reality. Years ago, I was divinely instructed, "A closed mouth will lead to a closed destiny." As stated in Luke 6:45, *"Out of the abundance of the heart, the mouth speaks."* Although our heavenly Father is aware of our desires, He insists that we ask before receiving (Matthew 6:8). Through our desires (visualization) and declarations (prayer), we come into agreement with God.

Job 22:28-29 elucidates, *"you will also declare a thing, and it will be established for you; So light will shine on your ways. When they cast you down, and you say, 'Exaltation will come!' Then He will save the humble person."* These verses attest to the potent force of declarations.

Additionally, in Job 38:12-13, God asked Job, *"Have you commanded the morning since your days began, and caused the dawn to know its place, That it might take hold of the ends of the earth, and the wicked be shaken out of it?"* In essence, God was telling Job how the mornings of our lives are given direction. Nothing takes shape without it being directed by the words from the mouth of an authority or a powerful person. Words must be spoken before we can see a performance.

The Power of an Authority's Declarations

God reaffirms only the words proclaimed by His servant, an authorized individual (Isaiah 44:26-28). The Prophet Isaiah elaborates on this, stating, *"...Who says to Jerusalem, 'You shall be inhabited,' to the cities of Judah, 'You shall be built,' and I will raise up her waste places; Who says to the deep, 'Be dry! And I will dry up your rivers'; Who says of Cyrus, 'He is My shepherd, and he shall perform all My pleasure, saying to Jerusalem, "You shall be built," and to the temple, "Your foundation shall be laid."* Without the declaration from God's servant, nothing transpires.

Declare in Alignment with God's Word

In Genesis 1, the Spirit of God was brooding (visualizing) over the face of the waters before God commanded, *"Let there be light"* and there was light. This principle was imparted to Joshua after Moses passed, at a time when Joshua likely felt daunted by the prospect of succeeding a prophet like Moses. One piece of divine counsel offered to Joshua for his success and prosperity involved declaring the Word both day and night (Joshua 1:8). The period God spent hovering over the waters allowed Him to carefully assess the situation and decide on the appropriate action. This means that declarations must align with God's will and Word. Joshua was advised not merely to utter feel-good phrases but to proclaim the Word of God. This principle is further solidified in 1 John 5:14, *"Now this is the confidence that we have in Him, that if we ask anything according to His will, He hears us.*

And if we know that He hears us, whatever we ask, we know that we have the petitions that we have asked of Him."

Aligning with God's will is crucial for remaining under the Lord's authority and guidance. The distinction between Lucifer and a person who meditates in God's way lies in alignment; unlike Lucifer, who declared his own desires irrespective of God's will, we seek harmony with God by steadfastly declaring His will. God's will is revealed through His Word! Start engaging with the Word of God with an open heart and mind.

4
Mysteries of Darkness

The concept of darkness is multifaceted. Darkness means many things to many people. Some are afraid of it, while some crave it. Some summon it, while others repel it. Some look forward to it, while others disdain it. All through the scriptures, we see a varied view of what darkness is and what believers are meant to do about it. While at the surface level, darkness can be seen mainly as the absence of light, we are exploring the deeper spiritual context of darkness.

Darkness in Meditation

You might be wondering what connection darkness has with meditation. In this book, I described meditation as a journey we embark on, accompanied by light, where we pass through darkness to arrive at a brighter light. Whether you believe you are looking up to God in heaven or God within you, there is a journey you will embark on that will involve passing through enemy territory.

Remember, the Bible says that Jesus Christ has been seated far above principalities and powers, and we have been made to sit with Him in heavenly places (Ephesians 1:20-21; 2:6). If Jesus is seated far above principalities and powers, and we are seated with Christ, it means that we are also seated far above principalities and powers. When we meditate and begin to feel darkness, it's typically because we walk through the darkness to arrive at the light, where Jesus Christ is.

There is a component of fear that is involved in meditation. Those who have meditated for a long time might have gotten so used to the fear that sometimes occurs that they might have forgotten it even exists. You can exercise your practical dominion over fear using the weapons of faith, love, and a sound mind (2 Timothy 1:7). Understanding that journey through darkness that often occurs in meditation will shield your heart from any fear of meditation.

21 Mysteries of Darkness

To further explain the concept of spiritual darkness, I will share 21 mysteries of darkness. I pray that the Holy Spirit gives you more insight into these mysteries so you can gain mastery over the devil's hiding place.

Mystery 1: Darkness has a right to exist where there is no light

God never banned or destroyed it.

In the beginning God created the heavens and the earth. The earth was without form, and void; and darkness was on the face of the deep. And the Spirit of God was hovering over the face of the waters. Then God said, "Let there be light"; and there was light. And God saw the light, that it was good; and God divided the light from the darkness. God called the light Day, and the darkness He called Night. So the evening and the morning were the first day. (Genesis 1:1-5)

Mystery 2: Darkness is present everywhere there is no light

All you have to do to introduce darkness into a domain is to turn off the light. The moment an enlightened person refuses to allow their lights to shine, darkness will be automatically permitted to take over. (Genesis 1:1-5)

Mystery 3: You cannot overcome darkness without passing through it

God said, *"When you pass through the waters, I will be with you; And through the rivers, they shall not overflow you. When you walk through the fire, you shall not be burned, nor shall the flame scorch you."* (Isaiah 43:2) The fire and rivers here signify darkness. Even God had to interact with darkness before He overcame it by bringing light into the picture.

God himself moved through darkness before He created light.

In the beginning God created the heavens and the earth. The earth was without form, and void; and darkness was on the face of the deep. And the Spirit of God was hovering over the face of the waters. (Genesis 1:1-2)

Mystery 4: Darkness is strong enough to be a prison

The power that darkness has to trap individuals is palpable.

Those who sat in darkness and in the shadow of death, Bound in affliction and irons— Because they rebelled against the words of God, And despised the counsel of the Most High, Therefore He brought down their heart with labor; They fell down, and there was none to help. Then they cried out to the Lord in their trouble, And He saved them out of their distresses. He brought them out of darkness and the shadow of death, And broke their chains in pieces. (Psalms 107:10-14)

Additionally, we see in Isaiah 42:7 that those in darkness are in a prison house.

"To open blind eyes, To bring out prisoners from the prison, Those who sit in darkness from the prison house."

Mystery 5: Darkness possesses the ability to create horror and fear

Where darkness exists, horror and fear will exist. Except when deliberately dominated, every darkness will have the ability to cause horror and fear.

"Now when the sun was going down, a deep sleep fell upon Abram; and behold, horror and great darkness fell upon him." (Genesis 15:12)

Mystery 6: Darkness is a hiding place for generational and valuable treasures

The only problem with treasures of darkness is, "Who is giving it to you?" While it is a problem to receive treasures of darkness from the devil, getting them from God is not a problem.

"I will give you the treasures of darkness And hidden riches of secret places, That you may know that I, the Lord, Who call you by your name, am the God of Israel." (Isaiah 45:3)

When God is the one giving you treasures of darkness, allow Him to provide them to you on His own terms. God desires to give us secret things.

"He reveals deep and secret things; He knows what is in the darkness, And light dwells with Him." (Daniel 2:22)

"Then you shall see and become radiant, And your heart shall swell with joy; Because the abundance of the sea shall be turned to you, The wealth of the Gentiles shall come to you." (Isaiah 60:5)

Many valuable things have been taken from the body of Christ and hidden in darkness. Valuable things like meditation have been hidden in darkness, and those who attempt to connect with such insights are stigmatized. As you mature in Christ, do not be satisfied with shallow explanations of why biblical practices should not be followed.

Mystery 7: Darkness is a weapon that can be controlled

While many people are afraid of darkness, you have to remember that it is a domain that can and should be controlled. Even though a child of God should not dwell in darkness, they should have dominion (control) over what happens there. Darkness can be ruled, it doesn't have to be governed by the devil. Do you always desire to disarm darkness, leave it to be occupied again, and then come to disarm it again? Why not instead continually rule over darkness? Ephesians 6:12 shows that there are *"...Rulers over the darkness of this age."* Daniel demonstrated this by being *"...chief of the magicians, astrologers, Chaldeans, and soothsayers."* (Daniel 5:11)

Mystery 8: Darkness has the capacity to make its inhabitants stumble

Darkness also causes delay because of the absence of light. A person in darkness does not see where they are going and stumble. Proverbs 4:19 states that a wicked person is in darkness and will stumble. This same darkness was mobilized against the Egyptian army when they went after the Israelites into the Red Sea. As a result of the darkness, the Egyptians kept stumbling in the Red Sea and did not catch up to the Israelites. Jesus echoed this sentiment when He said, *"...the one who walks in darkness does not know where they are going."* (John 12:35)

Mystery 9: Darkness is a hiding place

God hid in darkness. In Psalms 18:11, God *"...made darkness His secret place; His canopy around Him was dark waters and thick clouds of the skies."* If God hides in darkness, it means there are valuable things in darkness. You simply shouldn't dwell in darkness. At the beginning of Jesus' ministry, you will see that He was unable to hide in darkness like His heavenly Father was able to. You will see that Jesus was discovered even when He didn't want to be known. In Luke 4:31-35, Jesus had to rebuke a demon-possessed man who was announcing Him when He was not ready to be revealed. You will notice that as Jesus grew in wisdom and stature (Luke 2:52), no demon-possessed person was able to identify who Jesus was until He was ready to reveal Himself.

Then He went down to Capernaum, a city of Galilee, and was teaching them on the Sabbaths. And they were astonished at His teaching, for His word was with authority. Now in the synagogue there was a man who had a spirit of an unclean demon. And he cried out with a loud voice, saying, "Let us alone! What have we to do with You, Jesus of Nazareth? Did You come to destroy us? I know who You are—the Holy One of God!" But Jesus rebuked him, saying, "Be quiet, and come out of him!" And when the demon had thrown him in their midst, it came out of him and did not hurt him. (Luke 4:31-35)

Mystery 10: Darkness is where those who do dark deeds dwell

The works of darkness are also known as the works of the flesh.

Now the works of the flesh are evident, which are: adultery, fornication, uncleanness, lewdness, idolatry, sorcery, hatred, contentions, jealousies, outbursts of wrath, selfish ambitions, dissensions, heresies, envy, murders, drunkenness, revelries, and the like; of which I tell you beforehand, just as I also told you in time past, that those who practice such things will not inherit the kingdom of God. (Galatians 5:19-21)

It is important to remember this because some might not know that their lifestyle gives darkness the power to oppress them. We must do all we can to avoid walking in darkness. The great light is available to you. Embrace Jesus Christ, the Light today!

"The people who walked in darkness Have seen a great light; Those who dwelt in the land of the shadow of death, Upon them a light has shined." (Isaiah 9:2)

Mystery 11: Darkness has power

Just like light is powerful, darkness also has power. We have seen that darkness can bring horror and fear. Darkness can also cause people to stumble. Do not play around with darkness. It has the power to suck people in and keep them trapped.

"He has delivered us from the power of darkness and conveyed us into the kingdom of the Son of His love [.]" (Colossians 1:13)

"When I was with you daily in the temple, you did not try to seize Me. But this is your hour, and the power of darkness." (Luke 22:53)

Mystery 12: There is light in darkness and darkness in light

Everywhere you see light, understand that darkness is potentially present. Everywhere you see darkness, understand that light can emanate from it. Jesus implored us to make sure that *"...the light in us is not darkness."* (Luke 11:35) We were all given light by Jesus Christ when we came into the earth (John 1:9), but we are to ensure that the light does not become darkness. Likewise, there is death in life and life in death.

Mystery 13: We all engage in darkness unknowingly

But we must cast it off as we grow in knowledge and wisdom. In Romans 13:12, we are told that *"The night is far spent, the day is at hand. Therefore let us cast off the works of darkness, and let us put on the armor of light."* In this context, darkness refers to ignorance, which is typically associated with darkness.

We are instructed to grow in light so we can desist from behaviour rooted in ignorance. Apostle Paul characterized that situation by saying, *"When I was a child, I spoke as a child, I understood as a child, I thought as a child; but when I became a man, I put away childish things."* (1 Corinthians 13:11) As a child grows, the child is expected to act honourably and wisely.

Mystery 14: Darkness traps those with an inability to see properly

Darkness easily traps those with bad eyes, i.e., without discernment, and hence, they lack the ability to see ahead and make course corrections where necessary. Luke 11:34 explains that the presence or absence of darkness in a person's life can be traced to the state of the eyes.

"The lamp of the body is the eye. Therefore, when your eye is good, your whole body also is full of light. But when your eye is bad, your body also is full of darkness."

If the discernment is good, there will be light, whereas if the discernment is lacking, there will be darkness.

King Solomon further clarified this when he stated that wisdom will enable a person to walk in light, while the one who lacks wisdom will walk in darkness. Learning is a powerful way to escape the darkness that is bred in ignorance. Do not yield to the lie that ignorance is bliss. Anyone who convinces you that something is too hard to learn wants to keep you trapped in darkness.

"The wise man's eyes are in his head, But the fool walks in darkness. Yet I myself perceived That the same event happens to them all." (Ecclesiastes 2:14)

Mystery 15: The end result of darkness is death

Remember that the devil's mission statement is to, *"...steal, kill, and destroy."* (John 10:10) Whenever the kingdom of darkness takes hold of a person, the end result is death. The spirit of death reigns and travels in darkness. The realm of darkness is also referred to as the shadow of death.

"He brought them out of darkness and the shadow of death, And broke their chains in pieces." (Psalms 107:14)

When Jesus was on the cross and was about to die, the spirit of death showed up, as represented by the darkness over the whole land. A few hours after this darkness took over the whole land, Jesus breathed His last breath.

Now when the sixth hour had come, there was darkness over the whole land until the ninth hour. And at the ninth hour Jesus cried out with a loud voice, saying, "Eloi, Eloi, lama sabachthani?" which is translated, "My God, My God, why have You forsaken Me?" Some of those who stood by, when they heard that, said, "Look, He is calling for Elijah!" Then someone ran and filled a sponge full of sour wine, put it on a reed, and offered it to Him to drink, saying, "Let Him alone; let us see if Elijah will come to take Him down." And Jesus cried out with a loud voice, and breathed His last." (Mark 15:33-37)

Mystery 16: Anyone who has not believed in Christ is in darkness

Regardless of how friendly, loving, etc., an unbeliever is, so long as they have not accepted Jesus Christ as their Lord and Saviour, they are in darkness. Unbelievers naturally walk in darkness, while believers walk in light. This is evident in the scriptures

"Do not be unequally yoked together with unbelievers. For what fellowship has righteousness with lawlessness? And what communion has light with darkness?" (2 Corinthians 6:14)

"You are all sons of light and sons of the day. We are not of the night nor of darkness." (1 Thessalonians 5:5)

Mystery 17: The darkness in a locality must be dominated to succeed

In Psalms 18:9, we see that even God *"...bowed the heavens also, and came down with darkness under His feet."* Darkness is your enemy. Make sure you pursue darkness and overtake it if you want to succeed. For example, it will be almost impossible for a ministry to thrive in an environment if you have not taken dominion over the forces of darkness in that domain. King David said in Psalms 17:37-39,

I have pursued my enemies and overtaken them; Neither did I turn back again till they were destroyed. I have wounded them, So that they could not

rise; They have fallen under my feet. For You have armed me with strength for the battle; You have subdued under me those who rose up against me.

Mystery 18: Darkness can be eliminated, subdued, and dominated by light

The brighter the light, the stronger the dominion it will have over darkness. In Genesis 1:16, we see that *"God made two great lights: the greater light to rule the day, and the lesser light to rule the night..."* No matter how dark your environment or situation is, if you grow the light (insight) you have about that situation, the darkness will dissipate. Do not fear the darkness in your domain, keep growing your light and you will watch the darkness leave you.

"For You will light my lamp; The Lord my God will enlighten my darkness." (Psalms 18:28)

"And the light shines in the darkness, and the darkness did not comprehend it." (John 1:5)

"Then I saw that wisdom excels folly As light excels darkness." (Ecclesiastes 2:13)

Mystery 19: Darkness can be heavy and bring about heaviness

One of the ways you know you are surrounded by darkness is the heaviness you experience. This heaviness can be physical, mental, emotional, etc. Heaviness is the feeling that you are carrying something more than yourself. Emotional heaviness is what results in depression. In Exodus 10:21-23, Moses obeyed the Lord's instruction to invoke darkness over Egypt. This darkness was so dark that it could be felt, and the people did not get up from their place. The Egyptians must have felt heavy and stuck.

Then the Lord told Moses, "Stretch out your hand toward heaven, that there may be darkness over the land of Egypt, darkness which may even be felt." So Moses stretched out his hand toward heaven, and there was thick darkness in all the land of Egypt three days. They did not see one another; nor did anyone rise from his place for three days. But all the children of Israel had light in their dwellings. (Exodus 10:21-23)

Mystery 20: The Word of God has the power to disarm darkness

This pertains to both the written and revealed Word of God. This was confirmed in 2 Peter 1:19, *"And so we have the prophetic word confirmed, which you do well to heed as a light that shines in a dark place, until the day dawns and the morning star rises in your hearts [.]"*

Jesus' death on the cross gave Him power over darkness. Indeed, *"Having disarmed principalities and powers, He made a public spectacle of them, triumphing over them in it."* (Colossians 2:15) Jesus' death on the cross is what made the Word of God become a two-edged sword in the hands of a believer.

We know that Jesus is the Word who became flesh and dwelt among us (John 1:14). Use the word of God confidently in battle and watch the darkness dissipate.

Mystery 21: The voice of God is the loudest in darkness

Within the prophetic, the nighttime is synonymous with locating the voice of God. The prophet Micah delivered a rebuke and punishment to the fake prophets by saying the normal prophetic course would no longer work for them. The divination they typically got from darkness will no longer come.

"Therefore you shall have night without vision, And you shall have darkness without divination; The sun shall go down on the prophets, And the day shall be dark for them." (Micah 3:6)

Moses narrated to the children of Israel that the voice of God came very loudly within the thick darkness. Meditation gives you access to the voice of God very loudly. Do your best to persevere in meditation until you begin to hear God's voice from deep within you.

"These words the Lord spoke to all your assembly, in the mountain from the midst of the fire, the cloud, and the thick darkness, with a loud voice; and He added no more. And He wrote them on two tablets of stone and gave them to me." (Deuteronomy 5:22)

5

Distractions in Meditation

A distraction is something that diverts your mind from where it should be. In contrast, focus is the opposite of distraction. A focused person is engrossed in a task, a thought, a person, etc., and consciously tries to maintain their attention on it. On the other hand, a distracted person is preoccupied with many things simultaneously. Meditation is about concentrating on a light source as we seek to draw light from it. The brighter the light, the more virtue we can draw from it. The sharper the focus, the more we can extract from the light. The light source Christians draw from is Jesus Christ in the many available forms.

The main hindrance to meditation can be termed distractions, which can be internal or external. Internal distractions may be mental, emotional, physical, etc., while external distractions can arise from technology, food, substance use, conversation, sin, etc.

INTERNAL DISTRACTIONS

Fear

Meditation has been shrouded in mystery within Christendom for many years, leading many within the body of Christ to be deceived into believing that all meditation is evil and unscriptural. Unfortunately, this mystery surrounding meditation has resulted in many Christians becoming afraid of it. Fear of meditation can be examined from two perspectives: **The Cognitive** and **The Spiritual.**

The Cognitive

The cognitive aspect of fear can often be addressed simply by becoming informed about the truth. When gaining knowledge of the truth does not allay a believer's concerns about meditation, it becomes apparent that the fear has spiritual roots. Consider a person who remains afraid that the liquid in a bottle is acid, even after seeing someone else drink from it without suffering any consequences. Similarly, some people's fear of meditation has been so deeply institutionalized that even after being shown unequivocal proof of meditation's biblical basis, they remain unconvinced.

What are you afraid will happen to you as a result of meditation? Are you concerned that you might find yourself in a spiritual realm and be unable to return to "reality"? Do you worry that meditation might jeopardize your salvation? Are you concerned that Jesus will be displeased with you for meditating? Or are you afraid that you might inadvertently adopt elements of Eastern religions like Buddhism, Hinduism, or Sikhism? Remember that Jesus Himself said,

Or what man is there among you who, if his son asks for bread, will give him a stone? Or if he asks for a fish, will he give him a serpent? If you then, being evil, know how to give good gifts to your children, how much more will your Father who is in heaven give good things to those who ask Him! (Matthew 7:9-11)

Fear is present anytime we embark on something different from our usual routines. It can easily emerge as we expose ourselves to new frontiers. A wise person once said, "Anytime fear is at the door, send faith to open the door." Faith is the virtue that results from the genuine manifestation of power, love, and a sound mind. When you meditate using the Word of God, as demonstrated at the Hour of Meditation, there is nothing to fear. Wouldn't it be odd to fear singing praise songs to God or reading the books of the Bible? I command every fear holding you back from meditation to be broken in Jesus' name.

The Spiritual

The spiritual nature of fear can only be addressed by invoking spiritual tools. The Bible tells us, *"...the weapons of our warfare are not carnal, but mighty in God."* (2 Corinthians 10:4) According to 2 Timothy 1:7, the weapons for dealing with the spirit of fear include power, love, and a sound mind.

"For God has not given us a spirit of fear, but of power and of love and of a sound mind."

Power

Power is the enablement that comes from the Holy Spirit to resist the barrier fear attempts to place in our path. Fear seeks to cripple a person's ability to act, while power enables them to take action. Fear constructs a mental prison, whispering, "What if?" In contrast, the spirit of power equips the fearful with a "So what?" attitude, propelling them forward. Fear establishes resistance to progress, but power dismantles obstacles to motion. Power is gained by connecting with God through grace channels. These channels include prayer, worship, meditation, faith in the Word, and fellowship. Facing fear is engaging in spiritual warfare, and power is essential to triumph in spiritual battles.

Love

Love is also a weapon for dealing with fear. Love generates the energy needed to confront the limitations fear attempts to impose on a person. Do you realize that when you are doing what you love or doing something for someone you love, you always find a way to deal with the challenges you face? The Bible tells us that *"Love never fails."* (1 Corinthians 13:8) Love puts us in a posture that will make it impossible for us to fail. This might be hard to believe because this is not many people's reality, but it is the truth. Walking in love towards God, yourself, and others will make your mind always find a way out of situations that would have trapped others.

Imagine if you were afraid of dogs, but you needed to access your doctor's home urgently, where a dog resides; otherwise, a loved one's life might be in danger. Do you think the fear of dogs will hold you back? If you genuinely love that person, you will see yourself running towards that house. A heart filled with love is a heart filled with the kryptonite against fear. Remember that perfect love casts out fear! (1 John 4:18) Continue to work on perfecting your love life, and you'll see that fear will be driven far away from you.

Sound Mind

A sound mind is simply right thinking. There is a way you will think that will expose the irrationality of fear and thereby dislodge it from your life. I once received a question from someone about how she was afraid of having encounters during meditation because she was not sure she would return to consciousness. My response to her was, "How do you return to consciousness every morning when you wake up from sleep?" An aha moment will come when you realize that some things you have been afraid of make no sense. The same God who has been preserving and waking you up every morning can bring you back into consciousness after every meditation session.

To operate in a sound mind, ask yourself, "What is the truth in this situation?" For example, you might have heard the admonition not to whistle because it invites snakes. You must ask yourself, "Where will the snakes come from?" Yes, whistling can summon snakes, but it's in a snake-prone environment. Operating in a sound mind will help you examine a thought's reasonability before it becomes a belief system.

Worry

Worry is negative meditation. It cripples our ability to meditate. Do not worry; worry leads to doubt, while meditation leads to faith. A person consumed by worry will focus on formlessness. They may say or think things like, "Look at how formless this *thing* is! Look at how empty this is! Look at how dark this place is." However, the more you do that, the more you'll find yourself worrying since what we focus on or give our attention to multiplies. For example, imagine someone unable to pay their rent and wanting to meditate on the situation. They can either dwell on the fact that they cannot pay their rent or ask God how little they have can be multiplied. One scenario epitomizes worry, while the other exemplifies meditation.

The Result of Worrying

Worry will have a person thinking about the fact that they cannot pay their rent, how the landlord will bang on their door with the sheriff accompanying them to pack all of their things, leaving them disgraced and ashamed as bystanders watch the situation unfold. The more you go in this direction, the heavier you will become, eventually leading you into a paralytic state. Meditation, however, will lead a person to look unto God, asking, 'How can this money be provided?' instead of focusing on what they don't have or the negative outcomes. So, in a nutshell, what meditation does is allow us to focus on God, which, as explained above, is the source of the solution to the problem.

The Bible tells us in Matthew 6:25 not to worry. Worry and anxiety lead to doubt, while meditation leads to faith. I have said before that the more you meditate on 'no way,' the sooner you'll realize that the 'no' can be removed so you can see the 'way.' Let's take a moment to break down the contents of Matthew 6:25-33.

Therefore I say to you, do not worry about your life, what you will eat or what you will drink; nor about your body, what you will put on. Is not life more than food and the body more than clothing? Look at the birds of the air, for they neither sow nor reap nor gather into barns; yet your heavenly Father feeds them. Are you not of more value than they?

God Promises to Take Care of You

Let's shift gears and look at something very interesting in the book of Genesis. When God created Adam and Eve and placed them in the Garden of Eden, did He not already provide them with food, work, companionship, clothing, and much more? Think about that momentarily, and then think about that problem that once consumed you. Is God not the same yesterday, today, and tomorrow? Will He not provide for you in the same manner?

Therefore do not worry, saying, 'What shall we eat?' or 'What shall we drink?' or 'What shall we wear?' For after all these things the Gentiles seek. For your heavenly Father knows that you need all these things. (Matthew 6:31-32)

Saying these things displays a lack of faith since the mouth speaks out of the abundance of the heart. If we know that we are kept by God and not only does He know we need all these things but can and will provide them, why is there worry? Imagine an infant knowing they have a loving mother who has an abundance of milk specifically for them, yet still worrying about what they'll eat, if they'll eat on time, and if it will be sufficient. Sounds unreasonable, right? Yet we do this day in and day out.

In this scripture, the Bible says that our heavenly Father knows what we need, not what we want. But most people often run to Psalms 23:1, saying, *"The Lord is my Shepherd, I shall not want."* Some fail to realize that scripture does not apply to everyone and every situation. This is for those who are under the authority of the Shepherd. The Bible tells us in Matthew 5:45 that "He makes His sun rise on the evil and the good, and sends rain on the just and on the unjust," meaning that rain falls on everybody. Everyone in the Kingdom of God will have their needs met, but only those under authority will have their wants also met.

Wants Vs. Needs

So, what is a want and a need? A need is something necessary to live and function. So, without it, you are unable to live and function. On the other hand, a want is something nice to have but not necessary to keep you alive. They can improve the quality of life or fulfill our desires. The Bible tells us that our needs will be met as children of God. As for a want, however, God gives those things to those who are genuinely under His authority, not those who have just read the book "The Blessings of Being Under Spiritual Authority" yet haven't applied anything from it. It is for those who go when He says, "Go," and who come when He says, "Come." These people have died to their flesh and have surrendered their will unto God as Jesus did when He said in Luke 22:42, *"Father, if it is Your will, take this cup away from Me; nevertheless not My will, but Yours, be done."*

Since not everyone has reached the realm of having their wants met yet, let's focus on the needs. Your heavenly Father knows what you need; He knows how much food you need to keep you alive. Some of us are carrying unnecessary burdens due to worrying about things we should've never been worrying about. Can you imagine a student worrying every day before going to school, "Will the teacher teach us today?" Probably not, right?

Do Not Worry

This is an instruction, but how many of us still find ourselves worrying about life? Before having an understanding of the relationship between a predator and prey, I used to pity the prey when they were caught and would even pray, "Oh Lord, don't let the lion catch them," until one day, the Lord explained that He created them as food for the lion. So how much more us, as His children? Are we not of more value than they? Yet, as children of God, we still find ourselves victims of worry.

Jesus said to not worry about tomorrow because tomorrow has enough problems of its own, so you need to focus on today. If you focus on how valuable you are in God and to God, you'll find that not only will there be no need for worry, but that there will also be no room for it. You'll understand, "Because I am valuable, I will be kept by God."

Redirect Your Attention

If you expect a visitor, is your attention not on the door? If it is a thief, would you not direct your attention to the window or any expected place of entry? Will you not focus on the phone if you expect a call? So why, then, do we focus our attention on the problem when we are expecting an answer or a solution to a problem instead of focusing on the seed that can birth the answer?

If our attention is elsewhere, is it not possible that we can miss the phone call, thief, or visitor? How much more an answer from God if we are consumed with worry and negative thoughts instead of positioning ourselves to receive the answer when it comes?

*So why do you worry about clothing? Consider the lilies of the field, how they grow: they neither toil nor spin; and yet I say to you that even Solomon in all his glory was not arrayed like one of these. Now if God so clothes the grass of the field, which today is, and tomorrow is thrown into the oven, will He not much more clothe you, O you of [great] faith? (*Matthew 6:28-30)

The lilies are not stressed. They are not trying to keep up with the Joneses, comparing their dressing to another's to determine whose is better. We are sometimes so consumed with ourselves and doing things in our strength that we can forget the One who made it all to be in the first place. We say things like, "How am I going to pay my school fees?" or "How am I going to pay my rent?" Did God not send you to school or put you in that home? And if He did, will He not take care of you? Now, if you put yourself there, things are a bit different, and you need to ask for mercy.

Seek God's Kingdom

"But seek first the kingdom of God and His righteousness, and all these things shall be added to you." Matthew 6:33

Sometimes we can be so absorbed with ourselves and our challenges that we forget the essence of this verse. Remember, the previous verse says that our heavenly Father knows we need all these things. Many people stop there, though, and find themselves discouraged or offended by God when they don't see the fulfillment of verses 31-32 in their life. And this is why. We are charged to seek first the Kingdom of God and His righteousness. It is a cause-and-effect relationship, where seeking God's kingdom first triggers the things to be added to you. So, if you are not seeking His kingdom, there is no cause for the things to be added.

Remember in Matthew 14 that Peter began to walk on water, but the moment he shifted his focus from Jesus to the storm, he began to sink. Similarly, we begin to sink when we focus on proverbial storms and challenges instead of seeking the Kingdom. An employer, for instance, knows that you need a paycheck at the end of your workweek. You should not worry about when or if you'll be paid. Instead, you should focus on doing the job you have been hired to do, and the paycheck will inevitably come. But many of us are not doing the job we have been called to but expect a paycheck. Can you imagine that? But that will no longer be your story, in the name of Jesus!

Enjoy and Live in the Present

Instead of living in the moment, some people are already 30 years into the future, worrying about the state of the world, if there will even be a world, the food crisis and shortages, and what they will do. But God is telling us in the above scripture not to worry about these things. Some of you may ask, "So, do I not plan for the future?" Planning for the future in accordance with God's will for your life is entirely different from worrying about what the future holds.

"Which of you by worrying can add one cubit to his stature?" Matthew 6:27

This verse simply asks us what value worrying brings us. There is a quote that brings the above verse into perspective. It says, "Worrying does not take away tomorrow's troubles. It takes away today's peace." Can you change your circumstances by worrying?

As a first-year university student, I remember worrying about my final-year project. After finishing high school, I heard one of my uncles talking about his final university project and how hard it was. I said to myself, "How am I going to do this? I've not even entered university!" From year one, I had already begun asking people questions about how to select my final-year topic. One day, the Lord finally asked me, "What is wrong with you?" Some of us used to have a Ph.D. in worrying, but we called it planning. But no, it was worrying. Someone later told me to leave the worry of the final year project alone because the first three years will prepare me for my final-year project. It was hard because I had a Ph.D. in worrying, but because of that revelation and understanding, I eventually stopped worrying about it. Are you aware that certain individuals find it difficult to fully enjoy life because they fear the blessings they've prayed for may not endure? For instance, they pray for a spouse, and when that spouse arrives, they fret about the possibility of someone else stealing their partner away. Similarly, they may pray for a job, but they become anxious about losing it once they secure it.

Declarations Against Worry

Say to yourself: I will not worry again! I refuse to worry in the name of Jesus.

Some people around us are specialists in worrying. How will you know who they are? When you encourage them, they will not receive it. You can encourage them for hours, but at the end of everything, you'll hear them say, "Yeah, I know, I know, but..." The only way to deal with these people is to pray for them and give them space. Enjoy every day of your life with the understanding and assurance that if you have it today, make the best use of it today.

Repeat this to yourself: I declare that worry will not consume me! I reject worry in Jesus' name.

There are individuals among us who specialize in worrying. How do you identify them? When you encourage them, they don't accept it. You could offer encouragement for hours, yet they still respond with, "Yeah, I know, I know, but..." The only approach with these individuals is to pray for them while giving them space. Let's not be so preoccupied with worrying about tomorrow that we forget to embrace and savour today.

The Mind

The mind is the steering wheel of meditation. We use it to transition between realms in the spirit and on earth. However, the mind can easily be influenced. We must position ourselves correctly to envision what we want to create clearly. Moses understood how to generate miracles, but the Israelites only observed the miracles (Psalms 103:7). There are defined seasons of enhanced productivity in everyone's life. These seasons of enhanced productivity are what I call "mating time." Not every moment is optimal for sowing. We must examine ourselves and our patterns to identify when we are easily offended or excited. The seeds we sow in our hearts yield more exponential results during these times.

There is a significant difference between being hindered in meditation due to a mental challenge and meditating at the wrong times. Like any other tool, the mind must be properly utilized to achieve good results. The mind must be treated like a little child. It should be raised lovingly and firmly, just as a responsible parent raises a child. The more you discipline your mind, the better it will serve you in meditation and life.

Meditation is akin to taking medication, which can be administered in many ways. Medication can be ingested in various forms or injected into the body. You meditate when you engage with God without your voice being heard by others. Hannah's prayer in 1 Samuel 1:13 was meditative in nature. Just as Eli misjudged Hannah's meditative prayer, meditation continues to be viewed negatively by some in the church today.

"Hannah was praying silently, and though her lips were moving, her voice could not be heard. Eli thought she was drunk."

The world might not hear you while meditating, but your voice is still being heard on high. Your voice can be very loud in the spirit realm, even if it's not heard in the earthly realm. Due to the internal nature of meditation, it is crucial that there are no internal distractions that can rob you of the effectiveness of meditation. Your mind is very critical in meditation. You want to maintain a peaceful and calm mind to aid your meditative lifestyle. As you improve your mental capacity, your meditation will become increasingly effective.

EXTERNAL DISTRACTIONS

Substance Abuse

The use of substances can affect the way the human mind, body, and emotions work. Meditation can never be the same for folks who use substances like alcohol, marijuana, mushrooms, etc. These dangerous and addictive substances will cause the mind to be altered and can manipulate the meditation experience. What is put in the body can alter your mind, emotions and will. Since many of these substances already have psychotic abilities that cause hallucinations and delusions, the visualization component of meditation will be in overdrive. It can not be trusted as coming from God.

Just like we are told not to drink and drive, we are also not meant to consume addictive substances and meditate. If you use addictive substances to aid your meditation as some spiritual folks do, you will initially feel the ease in a "spiritual" connection. Still, you will experience a slump afterwards and eventually become dependent on it. Hence, addiction to substances will be deepened when you merge meditation with the use of addictive substances. If you are struggling with substance abuse, I declare you free now, in Jesus' name. That addiction holding you down loses its power over you now, in Jesus' name.

Food

The food we eat can affect the effectiveness of our meditation. Some foods have adverse effects on our body and must be well managed if you want to meditate properly. Can you imagine attempting to meditate while feeling bloated? One of the best times to meditate is when your body is quiet and peaceful. Meditation is enjoyable when you're not having headaches, pains, or any form of stress in the body. Study your body and adopt eating habits that work well for you. On a general and simplistic note, replacing alcohol, concentrated juices, etc., with water is advisable. Also, avoiding refined sugar will benefit your health and meditation adventure.

The relationship between food and meditation is about what you eat and drink and when you eat and drink. Meditation is best done on an empty stomach. The benefit from spiritual activity is exponentially increased on an empty stomach. You will get more results when you pray, worship, meditate, and study the word while fasting. You can still take advantage of the benefits of fasting while meditating just by meditating on an empty stomach. The lighter you are physically, mentally, and emotionally, the easier it will be to transcend spiritually.

Talking

Another distraction to meditation is obviously talking. A person who talks a lot will find it hard to focus and hence to meditate. There is time for everything under the sun. There is a time to talk and a time to refrain from talking. Excessive talking can drain the energy that is needed for meditation. This truth was validated in God's instruction to the Israelites when faced with the Wall of Jericho. God told them to refrain from talking for a few days as they marched around the wall of Jericho and to give a big shout on the seventh day. The energy that was saved was to be released on that seventh day. Meditation helps us to invest our energy by saving our words before we release the invested power in the form of declarations.

Now Jericho was securely shut up because of the children of Israel; none went out, and none came in. And the Lord said to Joshua: "See! I have given Jericho into your hand, its king, and the mighty men of valor. You shall march around the city, all you men of war; you shall go all around the city once. This you shall do six days. And seven priests shall bear seven trumpets of rams' horns before the ark. But the seventh day you shall march around the city seven times, and the priests shall blow the trumpets. It shall come to pass, when they make a long blast with the ram's horn, and when you hear the sound of the trumpet, that all the people shall shout with a great shout; then the wall of the city will fall down flat. And the people shall go up every man straight before him." (Joshua 6:1-5)

Technology

One of the most pervasive hindrances to meditation is technology. Tim Cook was quoted as saying that Apple did not make iPhones, so they are looked at all the time. The promise of technology was that it would make our lives better. Unfortunately, technology has done the opposite. Addictions have been multiplied by technology abuse; families are being damaged by technology abuse; overall quality of life is diminishing as a result of addiction to technology. Anyone who will put technology to good use must do so intentionally. In its native state, your phone is designed to take much of your time and attention.

How to Curb a Phone Addiction

Avoid Stress

Addressing the root cause of stress is essential for a healthier approach to managing one's life and well-being. When individuals tackle stress at its source, they may be less inclined to seek escapist behaviours, such as mindless scrolling through technology, to pass time. By confronting and resolving the issues that cause stress, individuals can reduce their reliance on technology for distraction, leading to more engaged, present, and fulfilling lives.

Remove Inbox Notifications

Continuously picking up and setting down your phone can lead to compulsive behaviour, significantly interfering with the peace required for effective meditation. I have taken proactive steps to combat these distractions by disabling all my notifications. This adjustment allows me to check messages and other communications on my terms, not merely in response to an alert, thereby minimizing concentration and activity disruptions.

It's advisable to turn off notifications for text messages, direct messages (DMs), emails, and other app alerts to prevent them from appearing on your home screen. I've even gone a step further by removing app-specific notifications, recognizing they, too, can serve as a mental diversion. Assess your phone usage: when you pick it up, are you immediately overwhelmed by a barrage of pending tasks and notifications? Controlling when and how you interact with your phone can cultivate a more serene, distraction-free environment conducive to meditation and mindfulness.

Remove Excess Alarms & Task Notifications

Some people have a series of alarms, calendars, and task notifications that should be removed. You want to ensure that when your phone beeps, it is for a valid reason. If you retain more reasons why your phone will beep unnecessarily, you will be training your mind to believe that there are times your phone will beep and you can ignore it. Simplicity aids meditation.

Unsubscribe from Marketing Email

If you are one of those people who receive lots of unnecessary marketing emails, ensure that you unsubscribe from as many of them as possible. These emails aim to get your attention, stimulate interest, activate your desire, and get you to act. That means that well-crafted marketing emails will disrupt your focus daily.

Delete Unnecessary Apps

Every app on your phone should have a purpose, and those no longer useful should be deleted. Knowing that you can always install an app when needed, you should streamline your phone use. One of the reasons many have become addicted to their phones is the diverse, sometimes unnecessary reasons for picking them up.

Streamline Social Media

Numerous research studies have linked the significant rise in anxiety, body insecurity, worry, and other mental health issues directly to the excessive use of social media. It's crucial to be honest with yourself regarding your social media habits. If you suspect that you've developed an addiction to social media, seeking assistance is a wise step. A practical beginning to addressing this issue could involve deleting your social media accounts and finding someone to hold you accountable.

Reflect on your reasons for using social media and strive to tailor your usage to fulfill those specific purposes only. Although social media platforms are designed to facilitate connections with like-minded individuals, they often become sources of noise and overwhelming distractions. One way to mitigate excessive social media use is by leveraging apps designed to monitor and limit screen time. A simple Google search for "screen time apps for iPhone/Android" can provide you with options for tools to help manage and regulate your phone usage effectively.

Gaming

Similar to social media, gaming has evolved into a highly addictive activity. While playing games is an enjoyable entertainment source, it can significantly disrupt a peaceful and meditative lifestyle. Implementing screen time regulation apps is an effective strategy for managing your gaming habits. Additionally, you can control your gaming on consoles by securing them in a locked space when not in use or even considering disposal if gaming has escalated into an addiction. Numerous games have the potential to warp an individual's sense of reality, which may impede their capacity to engage in effective meditation. Recognizing and addressing excessive gaming is essential for maintaining a balanced, focused, and meditative mind.

Create Healthier Habits

Incorporating meditation as the first activity in the morning and the last before bed can significantly contribute to establishing healthy habits. The practices we engage in upon waking and before falling asleep play vital roles in shaping our mental and emotional states. Adopting the routine of meditating during these times can significantly impact your capacity to recall dreams, spiritual visitations, or insights gained during meditation sessions.

To facilitate this healthier habit, consider reducing the immediate accessibility of your phone upon waking and before sleep. This can be achieved by using a traditional alarm clock instead of your phone's alarm functions and storing your phone away from your sleeping area, such as in your car or another room. This change discourages the immediate reflex to check messages or social media and encourages a more mindful and reflective start and end to your day through meditation.

6
Meditation Tools

YOUR NATURAL RHYTHM

Meditation is a tool for aligning ourselves with the natural rhythm God has etched in us. This might sound crazy, and you may wonder, "What is natural rhythm?" There's a natural pace God created you to flow in. It is your ebb and flow for speech, physical movement, and more. Meditation brings us back to that center point, making connecting with God easier. This is why people often say they feel centered after properly meditating. The natural rhythm I speak of can also be creatively understood as the "music within." The internal melody increases and decreases at different intensities and points in time. It is the pace or sound within that you lean into to connect with God or operate effectively. Awareness of your natural rhythm can help guide your discovery of various audible sounds or forms of music that can act as supportive mediums in meditation. Some people, like myself, have an internal rhythm aligned with their speaking pace. My rhythm, for example, is more steady-paced. As a result, I realized that I only needed to lean into that pace to meditate effectively, and my meditation became effortless.

Anointed Music

There are times, however, when I use piano instrumentals to aid the process. For music to be effective in meditation, it must be aligned with the natural rhythm God created you with. In meditation, each person must know what works best for them. The musical rhythm we use should vary depending on our situation. We must find our rhythm; once we are quiet, we can engage in visualization.

So, if you try to meditate at the pace that I meditate, you'll quickly become frustrated. You may realize that you need something slower or faster. Once you try it, you will understand what I am talking about. Some people naturally move at a faster pace. Some listen to solemn music, while others need faster music to connect in meditation. I can reckon that most evangelists would need certain types of songs, possibly at a faster pace, and that is how it should be.

It may take time to discover your natural ebb and flow but do not be discouraged. Thomas Edison said that although he didn't know the solution, he knew that 10,000 options weren't the solution. A good place to start the journey can be to identify the sounds and rhythms that disrupt your meditation. Another starting point can be to explore different instruments.

External Environment

To be quiet does not necessarily mean the absence of sound. For some individuals, the ideal setting for quiet time is amidst the hustle and bustle of a busy cafe during peak hours. This cafe environment mirrors some people's internal rhythm, placing them into a meditative state and enhancing their focus. Everyone possesses a natural rhythm with which they have been created. For those seeking to delve deeper into this concept, exploring the field of chronobiology is recommended. Chronobiology studies the various rhythmic patterns living organisms experience, influenced by light and temperature.

Earth's Elements

Numerous factors play a role in our reaction to the external environment. The most effective approach to deepening our understanding is through learning and observation. Rather than self-judgment or condemnation for reacting in less-than-ideal ways, seek forgiveness and examine the factors that led to your negative response. Life will be more beneficial and advantageous if we live it as a researcher instead of a judge.

The main elements on Earth are **climate and weather (wind), atmosphere (air), lithosphere (land), hydrosphere (water),** and **biosphere (living organisms on Earth).**

Climate and Weather (Wind)

Wind represents the dynamic movement of air within the atmosphere, a fundamental aspect of weather patterns and climate. The movement of air masses, influenced by factors such as temperature and pressure differences, contributes to wind generation.

Atmosphere (Air)

Earth's atmosphere, a vital gaseous layer, envelops our planet. Predominantly composed of nitrogen and oxygen, this layer is crucial for sustaining life, regulating climate, and influencing weather patterns.

Lithosphere (Land)

The Earth's solid surface, or lithosphere, encompasses the crust and the upper mantle's outer segment. It's characterized by diverse landforms, including mountains, valleys, plains, and other geological structures, shaping the planet's physical landscape.

Hydrosphere (Water)

The hydrosphere covers all Earth's water bodies—oceans, seas, lakes, rivers, groundwater, and atmospheric water vapour. Essential for life, it plays a pivotal role in climate regulation and the global water cycle.

Biosphere (Living Organisms on Earth)

The biosphere encompasses all living organisms and their interactions with the atmosphere, hydrosphere, and lithosphere. It is the sum of Earth's ecosystems and biodiversity. It represents the complex web of life, highlighting the interconnectedness of all living beings with their environment.

Each element plays a part in enhancing or negatively impacting our meditation experience. Remember that man is a spirit that functions within the limitations of the earth. Man's understanding of the rules on earth has enabled us to achieve several astounding accomplishments, including creating planes to fly, seemingly in violation of the law of gravity. Ignoring these principles in the name of faith is not a display of wisdom. A child of God must be open to learning and growing while avoiding anything that involves allegiance to the devil or his mission to steal, kill, and destroy.

It is known that there are people alive today who do not believe that "Western" education should be tolerated, such as Boko Haram. The unfortunate truth is that they use technology like vehicles, ammunition, communication devices, etc., invented, manufactured, and distributed using knowledge gathered through education to further their mission. Human beings are indeed fascinating!

Interacting with the External Environment

When people tell me they do not know how to meditate, I suspect they have been trying to emulate someone else's method and experiences rather than discovering what uniquely works for them as individuals.

Movement

For instance, my preferred setting for quietness is complete stillness. By stillness, I mean an absence of movement, distractions, etc. This is my preference. However, some people dislike absolute stillness because it ironically amplifies the noise in their minds. These individuals might be the ones who sleep with natural sounds in the background because it counterbalances the stillness within them.

For others, motion is necessary to foster a sense of quietness. These are the people who think more clearly in a moving vehicle. Have you noticed how some children fall asleep more easily during a drive than in the silence of their room? Similarly, some find pacing back and forth conducive to entering a meditative state, opening the door to deeper insight and thoughts. Your harmonious interaction with the earth's elements will influence the tranquillity of your internal environment.

Altitude

When the Bible mentions that Jesus went to pray on the mountain, it wasn't solely for the quietness but also because of the mountain's elevation. Scientifically, it's understood that ascending in altitude alters atmospheric pressure. While some experience discomfort and altitude sickness as they go higher in altitude, some thrive and feel more at peace as they go higher. Jesus seemed to be among those who felt more at peace with elevation.

Different geographical planes affect how meditative you feel. For some, the higher in the air they go, the better. For others, the closer to the ground they are, the better. For others, the faster they go physically, the better. For some others, the slower they go physically, the better. I've also observed that some individuals find being near or interacting with water enhances their meditation.

Light Vs. Darkness

External environments also include light exposure while meditating *(For further insight, please see the Mysteries of Darkness chapter)*. Just as there are different stages in the sleep cycle, there are deeper stages in the meditation cycle. During meditation, we journey in light (the Word), pass through darkness, and arrive at a brighter light. Where possible, the best environment for meditation should be a dark place. If you're unable to meditate in a dark space, perhaps due to work or other obligations, you can limit the amount of stimulants in your environment.

Anointed Environments

Moreover, some environments naturally possess a high spiritual "charge." Jacob journeyed from his father's house to Padan Aram, where he eventually met his wife, Rachel, illustrates this. He encountered a spiritually charged environment during his journey and recognized its significance. This encounter is detailed in the biblical account of his journey.

Now Jacob went out from Beersheba and went toward Haran. So he came to a certain place and stayed there all night, because the sun had set. And he took one of the stones of that place and put it at his head, and he lay down in that place to sleep. Then he dreamed, and behold, a ladder was set up on the earth, and its top reached to heaven; and there the angels of God were ascending and descending on it. And behold, the Lord stood above it and said: "I am the Lord God of Abraham your father and the God of Isaac; the land on which you lie I will give to you and your descendants. Also your descendants shall be as the dust of the earth; you shall spread abroad to the west and the east, to the north and the south; and in you and in your seed all the families of the earth shall be blessed. Behold, I am with you and will keep you wherever you go, and will bring you back to this land; for I will not leave you until I have done what I have spoken to you." Then Jacob awoke from his sleep and said, "Surely the Lord is in this place, and I did not know it." And he was afraid and said, "How awesome is this place! This is none other than the house of God, and this is the gate of heaven!" Then Jacob rose early in the morning, and took the stone that he had put at his head, set it up as a pillar, and poured oil on top of it. And he called the name of that place Bethel; but the name of that city had been Luz previously. (Genesis 28:10-19)

Negative and Positive Spiritual Forces

Jacob had the insight to recognize that negative spiritual forces can influence an environment and can also be spiritually charged positively, facilitating access for divine beings to operate freely. Meditating in a spiritually charged environment is profoundly different from meditating in an ordinary, or worse, negatively influenced environment. Jacob understood that his significant dream while sleeping in that location was not coincidental. This underscores the distinction between meditating in a genuine place of worship and meditating in a regular environment. It's crucial to be aware of the state of your environment and to optimize your space for meditation. I encourage you to leave environments that hinder a meditative practice and seek out those that support it.

Internal Environment

Posture

I previously wondered why people cross their legs and sit on a mat when meditating. Through my practice over time, I've realized that the strategic position of your body during meditation is a vital aspect of staying connected. I quickly realized that all body parts must be at ease to focus during meditation. The same measures taken to quiet one's mind and emotions must also be taken to position the body comfortably. Have you ever attempted to focus on something while in pain? If you have, you will attest to how difficult it may have been. You may find that your mind keeps going back to the pain point. However, overcoming the pain would position you for smooth meditation.

However, crossing your legs and sitting on a mat are not the only ways to comfortably position your body for meditation. I've discovered that, at times, laying down flat is a suitable position for meditation. The experience can be likened to when a person goes for a massage. The position adopted during a massage is strategic, not just for easy access to central parts of the body but also for relaxation. In some cases, you can find yourself in a meditative state.

Elijah

In 1 Kings 18:42, we see Elijah assuming a comfortable meditating position. I am going this deep because when I began to learn, I didn't find people I could learn from, especially within the body of Christ, yet these are things that the fathers in scripture were practicing. These are things that Elijah practiced. Do you realize that for Elijah to have his head between his legs, he had to have his legs crossed in a position similar to yoga? Many things have been taken from Christianity and misconstrued as a worldly practice. It is high time we take a stand to correctly represent the tools God has given us to connect with the divine. Feel free to assume a position that allows you to breathe properly and focus your mind while meditating.

Stable Emotions

Emotions can be one of the most challenging aspects to quiet and still. They often become the loudest when everything else seems to be hushed, especially at the beginning of meditation. Feelings of sadness, irritability, or uneasiness resurface when you desire to be quiet. Suddenly, you may start to remember all the people who angered you or caused you pain as you begin to meditate. This highlights the importance of walking in love daily, as it helps stabilize your emotions, which, in turn, aids in meditation. When you reach a point in meditation and recall what someone did to you, and you get angry, immediately exchange your ashes for beauty. Say, "Lord, I forgive this person." Do not let the anger fester in your spirit; otherwise, it will transform the time meant for meditation into a pre-meditation for anger, which is undesirable. Throughout meditation, you must maintain love in your heart.

Stable Mind

The world today has many means for achieving a "stable mind." Hypnosis is one of those means. What happens to a person in hypnosis is similar to what happens when a person gets deep into meditation. The essence of hypnosis is to bring a person into a sleep state, a state where they become zombie-like and can be controlled and made to do practically anything. They are put in a state where they are not struggling and are trusting, quiet, and susceptible to any input, command, or instruction.

This is similar to what we can bring ourselves into in meditation. The only difference is it is not an external person manipulating you. It is you giving control to the Holy Spirit so that you can get into that zone. This is why you need to have a timer when you meditate the right way, as some people can be in a meditative state for days, weeks, months, and even years. When all the factors and components that stimulate effective meditation are in place, meditation can automatically go on for a long time.

In that state, it's almost as if the body has been frozen and will not need food, water, or other essentials. For example, when we are excited, we can forget that we have not eaten. If forgetting to eat and not realizing the need to can be achieved by simply focusing or being preoccupied, how much more when you meditate with the understanding you have captured from this book?

Meditation is very powerful. God created it for His children to access the best of the best from Him. It might not be your primary channel of grace (*see my book on Channels of Grace for more insight*), but if you take the things you have read in this book and begin to put them into practice, perhaps a little while from now, you will meditate with ease and get extraordinary results.

A Meditative Lifestyle

For many years now, I have been meditating for many hours every single day. The same way you can be humming a song while engaging with people is the same way you can meditate on a word while talking to people. You will soon realize that you can be plugged in as you go about your day, so you will not be depleted in any way by the grace of God. It is good to have a scheduled time for meditation; otherwise, it would never happen. Some people's lifestyles make it easy for them because they are introverted, but it doesn't mean that only introverts can meditate excellently well.

How To Build a Stable Mind

Focus Your Attention

Do not attempt to focus by trying not to think about what you are thinking about. By trying not to think about something, you are already thinking about it. The best way to focus is by focusing on something in particular and gradually letting go of what you are focusing on. This is why some religions focus by utilizing prayer beads like rosaries. The Muslims call it tasbeeh or misbaha. This string of prayer beads is used for prayer, meditation, etc. Find something to focus your attention on. This is why people in those days had their rosaries and kept going through the parts of the cross as they went into meditation. So, you can focus on an object or item in your room or space. This is why pendants are used in hypnosis to get people into a state of focus. It will reach a point where nothing else is holding your attention but what you are looking at. Gradually, as you stop focusing on the item, you will realize that everything is quiet. Your eyes work this way. When you look at something so intently, you will lose sight of anything else around you. This kind of focus is the fastest way to quietness.

Reading

Reading helps us to focus. Discipline yourself to read for at least 10 minutes each day without distraction. Extend the amount of uninterrupted time you spend reading every day to improve your ability to focus. Imagine if you aim to read uninterrupted for one hour each day. This will untrain your mind from the constant task-switching approach we have imbibed over the years from jumping from one technology, inbox, or message to another.

Avoid Worry

Worry imbalances the mind and disrupts meditation. When you learn to live your life following Philippians 4:7-8, you will realize that when you get to a place of meditation, it will be easier to keep ascending because you're not worried or anxious about anything.

Anointed Words

Jesus made it clear that the words He spoke carry the power of the Holy Spirit (John 6:63). There are words you can hear that will set you in a meditative state. Many wonder why, no matter how well-rested they are, whenever they connect to the HoM, they fall into an unconscious meditative state. Remember, I stated earlier that meditation does not mean your thoughts must be silent. The mind can be ruminating on words that are in line with Philippians 4:8, "Finally, brethren, whatever things are true, whatever things are noble, whatever things are just, whatever things are pure, whatever things are lovely, whatever things are of good report, if there is any virtue and if there is anything praiseworthy—meditate on these things." Some people have become an embodiment of these words. Some people have disciplined themselves to focus on words that align with Philippians 4:8. When you hear words from such people, it will seem like you have already meditated.

Demonic Words

Every supernatural personality can draw you into the environment they came from. Hence, words from a venomous person will have disastrous consequences. You will hear words that can cause you to begin to operate out of character. One reason why Eve fell for the devil's schemes was because she spoke to the devil. The moment you start to speak to the devil, you will already begin to get drawn into the devil's illusive capacity. Remember that an illusion is a perception or interpretation of something that differs from reality. An illusion can be optical, auditory, and cognitive. In essence, having conversations with the devil or people with demonic inclinations will take you into the opposite of a meditative state.

Supernatural Encounters

Supernatural encounters can force you into a meditative state. Any supernatural personality that appears to you will bring you into a meditative state. If you encounter a supernatural personality from God, that personality will draw you into the aura of heaven. Likewise, if you encounter a demonic personality, that personality will seek to draw you into a demonic aura. Some people refer to aura as energy. However, I prefer "aura" instead of "energy." The moment an encounter starts, you will already be drawn into a different atmosphere. If it's a demonic encounter and you don't want to get sucked in, you will have to engage in spiritual warfare to restrict yourself from getting sucked into a demonic aura.

We will review a few supernatural encounters in scripture to get more insight.

Adam

In Genesis 2, God appeared to Adam before Eve was created. In verse 21, we see that Adam fell into a deep sleep. When Adam woke up, he saw that Eve had already been created. You see that in this situation, Adam did not need to initiate the process of quietness, visualization, and declaration. The supernatural encounter put Adam in a deep sleep, which then made him visualize his wife (Eve was created according to the blueprint and desires that God saw in Adam's heart), and eventually declare in verse 23, "…This is now bone of my bones and flesh of my flesh; She shall be called Woman, because she was taken out of Man." How did Adam know all the things he declared? It came through his meditation. This is why I let people know that you did not waste your meditation because you became unconscious (slept) while you meditated.

Abram

Abram had a particular encounter with God. God instructed Abram to offer a sacrifice to validate that he was going to possess the land. In verse 12, we are told, *"And when the sun was going down, a deep sleep fell upon Abram; and, lo, a horror of great darkness fell upon him."* Again, we see that Abram's encounter with God immediately put him in a meditative state. When God chooses to visit us, He accelerates our ability to meditate.

Abraham even built altars to represent his previous encounters with God. An altar is simply a way to capture an experience so it can remain ever-fresh. An altar does not have to be made of wood, etc. An altar can be a recording, a message, a picture, etc., in as much detail that depicts our experience with God. Abraham proved that while we should crave encounters with God regularly, we can still draw from previous spiritual encounters. We see in Genesis 13:4 that Abram went "...to the place where his tent had been at the beginning, between Bethel and Ai, to the place of the altar which he had made there at first. And there Abram called on the name of the Lord." While Abram trusted God for more visitation, he was using the past spiritual encounters well.

Daniel

Daniel had spiritual encounters that translated into meditation. He was enveloped in an encounter where an angel visited him, and that angelic encounter led to him falling into a deep sleep (Daniel 8:18). Also, in Daniel 10:9, Daniel recounts, *"Yet heard I the voice of his words: and when I heard the voice of his words, then was I in a deep sleep on my face, and my face toward the ground."* Again, this shows the power of supernatural encounters in getting us into a meditative state. The moment you have contact with a spiritual being, whether an angel or a human, you will bypass the need to engage in the meditation stages and be automatically carried deeper into meditation.

Systems

The only way to replicate success is to put it into a system. God made man once, but because of the system He put in place, man has been replicating and will continue to replicate until Jesus comes. Everything God made can reproduce as long as the right principles are engaged.

Here are some ideas for making meditation a part of your daily life:

1. Set aside time for meditation - quietness, visualization, and declarations.

2. Remove your phone notifications. This will enable you to operate with more focus and reduce daily mental distractions.

3. Go to bed meditating on the Word. Once you wake up, recollect what Word you were meditating on the previous night and resume meditating on it. If you don't put something of value in your spirit before you go to bed, you will wake up with junk.

4. Keep meditating on the Word until a scripture draws your attention. When you meditate next, focus on the scripture that draws your attention.

7

Frequently Asked Questions

There is a lot of mystery surrounding meditation that must be addressed to enjoy and benefit from meditation. In our exploration of the mystery of Christian meditation, we have delved deep into the essence of this sacred practice, seeking to uncover its profound significance in the lives of believers. Yet, as we reach the end of this book, it's essential to pause and reflect on the tangible impact meditation can have on our daily lives. In this chapter, we will examine real-life questions we received from individuals (through the meditation sessions that I host on YouTube) who have embraced Christian meditation allowing it to shape their spiritual journey and transform their spirit, soul, and body.

Falling Asleep or Becoming Unconscious

Countless people have expressed their frustration to me about falling asleep or going unconscious while meditating. Many people think their meditation was not successful because they do not remember what happened when they were meditating. The idea that your meditation was not successful because you fell asleep or went unconscious is absolutely wrong and can cause you to completely miss out on the advantages of meditation.

You become unconscious while meditating because the mind was put to sleep, not because you are unable to meditate properly.

Adam

Adam was put to sleep by God Himself when Eve was to be created (Genesis 2:21-23). In essence, Adam was put in a meditative state. The moment Adam woke up, he saw and understood what happened when he was unconscious. Even though you were not aware of what happened while you were meditating, it does not mean that nothing happened.

And the Lord God caused a deep sleep to fall on Adam, and he slept, and He took one of his ribs, and closed up the flesh in its place. Then, the rib which the Lord God had taken from man He made into a woman, and He brought her to the man. And Adam said: "This is now bone of my bones and flesh of my flesh; She shall be called Woman, because she was taken out of Man." (Genesis 2:21-23)

Abraham

The Bible also tells us that Abraham was put to sleep when he came in contact with God in Genesis 15:12. The power of God is able to put your mind to sleep during meditation. In some cases, you can be partially awake and partially asleep. In this scenario, you will be aware of what is happening in the physical and spiritual realms simultaneously without being able to interact with the physical realm.

Ensure that your focus is not on whether you are conscious or unconscious while meditating. Some people need the rest that meditation puts them in, especially if they decide to meditate before going to bed at night. One of the ways that the Lord gives His beloved rest is through meditation.

King David

In Psalms 4:8, King David alluded to being able to sleep in peace because the Lord made him dwell in safety. We also know that David shared that he was always meditating on his bed before sleeping. King David said, "When I remember You on my bed, I meditate on You in the night watches." (Psalms 63:6)

You will no longer need sleeping pills once you begin to meditate on your bed before sleeping.

Help, I Didn't See or Hear Anything

Another question that many people ask is why they did not see anything during meditation. Not everyone will see something while meditating, but everyone will become something as a result of meditation. You can never be the same person after interacting with a spiritual being. Let me remind you that Jesus is the word that became flesh (John 1:14). The word that became flesh is also full of life. The life we engage with during meditation is transmitted whether or not we see something or not.

The essence of meditation is not necessarily to see things in the spirit but to receive grace from God to do great things and become great people. It is sometimes interesting to hear people strive to hear from God but struggle to obey God. Sometimes, I meditate but do not see anything in the spirit. Do not make your meditation time with the Lord transactional. The goal of meditation is intimacy with Jesus.

Was that God or Me?

Another commonly asked question comes from those who saw or heard things during meditation. Many wonder if what they saw or heard originated from God or their own minds. There is a principle in the spiritual realm that is critical to understand: whoever you address your request to is the one who has the authority to respond. This is why Jesus instructed us to begin our prayers by addressing them to our Father in heaven (Matthew 6:9). If you are born-again and you directed your meditation to your Father in heaven, with the seed for visualization being God's word, the person of Christ, or the testimony of Jesus, then anything good that emerged from your meditation came from God.

How Do I Know My Meditation Session Was Effective?

Hearing from God

For many who engage in meditation, the experience of hearing from God is a central and transformative aspect of their practice. Through quiet contemplation and focused prayer, believers open themselves up to divine revelation, eagerly seeking to discern the voice of God speaking to their hearts. Conversations with those who have been practicing meditation reflect this profound encounter, with many reporting hearing from God during their meditation sessions. Whether through whispers of guidance, words of comfort, or insights into His word, the experience of hearing from God serves as a source of guidance, assurance, and spiritual nourishment for those who seek His presence.

Feeling Refreshed and Satisfied

The sense of refreshment and satisfaction that accompanies meditation is a testament to the restorative power of communion with God. Many have attested that engaging in meditation leaves them feeling refreshed, rejuvenated, and satisfied as they bask in the presence of their heavenly Father and find rest for their weary souls. In the stillness of meditation, believers find solace and peace as they are enveloped in the loving embrace of their heavenly Father, who restores their strength and renews their spirit.

Experiencing the Fruit of the Spirit

The fruit of the Spirit, as outlined in Galatians 5:22-23, is evident in the lives of those who engage in meditation. As believers cultivate a deeper intimacy with God through meditation, they bear witness to the transformative work of the Holy Spirit in their hearts and lives. Many who have joined me for the Hour of Meditation (in person or online) have reported experiencing peace, joy, love, and other fruits of the Spirit as a direct result of their meditation practice. Through the cultivation of spiritual disciplines such as meditation, believers are empowered to walk in the fullness of God's love, grace, and power, bearing witness to His presence and transforming work in their lives.

Peace and Clarity

Perhaps one of the most profound benefits of meditation is the experience of peace and clarity that it brings to the hearts and minds of believers. Perhaps one of the most testified benefits of meditation is that it serves as a source of inner peace, providing clarity amidst the chaos and confusion of life's trials and tribulations. In the presence of God, believers find refuge and strength as they are reminded of His sovereign care and steadfast love. Through meditation, believers are able to quiet their minds, center their hearts, and find peace in the midst of life's storms.

Increased Energy

Feeling energized after meditation is a common experience among believers who make it a regular part of their spiritual routine. Meditation is a source of spiritual nourishment and empowerment, invigorating the soul and renewing the mind. In the presence of God, believers find strength and vitality as they are infused with His divine energy and grace. Through meditation, believers are empowered to walk in the fullness of God's purposes and plans, as they are filled with His Spirit and equipped for every good work. Many people often report feeling energized, seeming like they have gotten many hours of sleep just from a one-hour meditation.

Ability To Focus on the Word and Prayers Throughout the Day

The practice of meditation has a profound impact on the daily lives of believers, as it serves to focus their minds and hearts on the truth of God's word and the power of the Holy Spirit. Meditation creates space for reflection and contemplation, allowing individuals to dwell deeply on the scriptures and engage in meaningful dialogue with their heavenly Father. Through meditation, believers are equipped to navigate the challenges of life with wisdom and discernment, as they are grounded in the truth of God's word and empowered by the Spirit to pray without ceasing.

Feeling Confident and Assured

The sense of confidence and assurance that accompanies meditation is a testament to the transformative power of communion with God. Many practitioners of meditation testify that engaging in meditation fosters a deep sense of trust and reliance on the promises of God, as believers are reminded of His faithfulness and provision. In the presence of God, believers find courage and strength as they are filled with His peace and confidence. Through meditation, believers are empowered to face life's challenges with boldness and assurance, knowing that their heavenly Father is with them every step of the way. This echoes King David's testimony in Psalms 23:4, "Yea, though I walk through the valley of the shadow of death, I will fear no evil; For You are with me; Your rod and Your staff, they comfort me." Meditation reinforces the reality of divine presence, which gives confidence and reassurance to the believer.

Feeling Love for God

The experience of feeling love for God is a natural outpouring of the deep intimacy and communion that believers experience in meditation. As believers engage in meditation, they are filled with a profound sense of love and adoration for their heavenly Father as they are overwhelmed by His goodness and grace. Meditation serves as a powerful reminder of God's unconditional love and faithfulness, as believers are reminded of His goodness and mercy. This love leads believers to find joy and excitement in the presence of God, for "In His presence is fullness of joy; At Your right hand are pleasures forevermore." (Psalms 16:11) Through meditation, believers are empowered to love God with all their heart, soul, mind, and strength, knowing that He first loved them and desires to be in a relationship with them.

Response to Triggering Emotions

Another profound benefit of meditation is its ability to help believers navigate the complexities of their emotions and experiences. Many have testified that meditation serves as a powerful tool for processing and responding to triggering emotions. Believers are guided by the wisdom and counsel of the Holy Spirit as they resolve emotionally complex situations. In the presence of God, believers find strength and courage as they are empowered to face their emotions with grace and resilience. Through meditation, believers are equipped to respond to triggering emotions with faith and trust, knowing that their heavenly Father is with them always and desires to bring healing and wholeness to their lives.

Feeling Lighter

The sense of feeling lighter after engaging in meditation is a testament to the transformative power of communion with God. As believers open themselves up to the presence of God, they are freed from the burdens and cares of life as they are filled with His peace and grace. In meditation, you experience liberation and release as you "cast you cares and burdens upon the Lord for He cares for you." (1 Peter 5:7) In the presence of God, believers find rest and renewal as they are filled with His presence and overwhelmed by His goodness and grace. Through meditation, believers are empowered to let go of the weight of the world and embrace the abundant life that God has promised them.

There is No Condemnation

For those who struggle with condemnation and self-doubt in their meditation practice, it is important to remember that God's grace is sufficient to cover all your shortcomings, pain, and failures. As believers engage in meditation, they are invited to come before the throne of grace with confidence, knowing that their heavenly Father delights in them and desires to draw them close.

Some may wrestle with feelings of unworthiness or inadequacy in their meditation practice, but it's important for you to remember that God's love is unconditional, and His mercy is boundless. Through prayer, reflection, and the support of fellow believers, they can find freedom from condemnation and experience the fullness of God's love and grace in their lives. Feeling condemned while meditating is often an indication that there is trauma that needs to be dealt with. Reach out to someone you can trust to help you deal with this trauma so your soul is purified.

Continue Persevering

While the majority of people report that they experience profound transformation and encounters through Christian meditation, it's important to acknowledge that not everyone may initially find it effective in their spiritual journey. Some people have shared that they have yet to experience the full benefits of meditation, perhaps struggling to connect with God in the stillness or wrestling with doubts and distractions. It's important for these individuals to recognize that Christian meditation is a deeply personal and individual practice and that the fruit of their meditation may take time to manifest. Through perseverance and faithfulness, they can continue to cultivate a deeper relationship with God through meditation, trusting that He will meet them in the quiet and lead them into greater intimacy with Him.

Whether through encounters with the Holy Spirit, moments of revelation and insight, or simply a deep sense of peace and joy, meditation serves as a powerful tool for spiritual growth and intimacy with God. May we continue to cultivate a deeper relationship with our heavenly Father through the practice of Christian meditation, trusting that He will meet us in the quiet and lead us into greater depths of His love and grace.

Epilogue

As we conclude our exploration of the profound topic of meditation, we are reminded of the vast depths and infinite possibilities that lie within this sacred practice. Through the journey we've embarked on in this book, we have delved into the essence of meditation, its significance in the Christian faith, and the transformative power it holds for those who engage in it with sincerity and reverence.

From the outset, we sought to unravel the multifaceted nature of meditation, understanding that it encompasses various forms and approaches, each with its own unique attributes and potential outcomes. Whether through quiet contemplation, visualization, or declaration, meditation offers a pathway to communion with God, transformation of the soul, and alignment with divine truth and purpose.

Through the lens of both Christian and non-Christian perspectives, we have discerned the critical distinctions between godly and ungodly meditation. We've recognized the inherent dangers of practices that seek to exalt self or spirits other than the Holy Spirit while also acknowledging the potential pitfalls of fear and skepticism that can hinder our embrace of meditation as a spiritual discipline.

Yet, amidst these challenges, we have discovered the profound promise and transformative potential of meditation. Drawing from the rich tapestry of biblical wisdom and spiritual insight, we have learned that meditation is not merely a passive exercise but an active engagement with the divine presence and truth. It is a sacred meeting between the believer, the Holy Spirit, and the Word of God—a place of potential agreement where creation, transformation, and power are unleashed.

As we reflect on the biblical foundations of meditation and its timeless relevance for the modern believer, we are inspired to embrace this ancient practice with renewed fervour and intentionality. We are called to cultivate a spirit of openness and receptivity to the voice of God, to align our hearts and minds with His truth, and to journey deeper into the mysteries of His love and grace.

In closing, may we carry forward the insights and revelations gleaned from our exploration of Christian meditation, allowing them to permeate every aspect of our lives and faith journeys. May we continue to seek God earnestly in the secret place of meditation, knowing that in His presence, we find healing, restoration, and transformation. May we walk in the fullness of His truth and power, empowered by the mystery of meditation, to live lives that honour and glorify His name.

Declare with me: From today, meditation will be easy for me! My meditation will be better! I will no longer struggle with meditation! I will meditate the right way, and it will be beneficial to me in the mighty name of Jesus! Amen!

For more practical steps in meditation, join me on my YouTube Channel (@Emmanuel Adewusi) today as we journey through meditation together!

Contact the Author

I know without a doubt that this book has been a blessing to you. I am looking forward to hearing your testimony.

You can stay connected with me through the following platforms:

Instagram: e.adewusi | **Youtube:** Emmanuel Adewusi
Website: emmanueladewusi.org

SUPPORT THE AUTHOR!

Review the Book on Amazon

A Sinner's Prayer

Dear Heavenly Father,

I come to You in the Name of Jesus Christ.

You said in Your Word, "Whosoever shall call upon the name of the Lord shall be saved." (Romans 10:13) I am calling on Your Name, so I know You have saved me now.

You also said that "if you confess with your mouth the Lord Jesus and believe in your heart that God has raised Him from the dead, you will be saved. For with the heart one believes unto righteousness, and with the mouth, confession is made unto salvation." (Romans 10:9-10) I believe in my heart Jesus Christ is the Son of God. I believe that He was raised from the dead for my justification, and I confess Him now as my Lord and Savior.

Thank you, Lord, because now, I am saved!

Thank You, Lord, because I know you have heard my prayer. Thank You, Lord, because I am now born again.

Signed _____

Date _____

About the Author

Apostle Emmanuel Adewusi is the Founding and Lead Pastor of Cornerstone Christian Church of God.

Called into ministry with the mandate to "bring restoration and transformation to all by teaching, preaching, and demonstrating the Gospel of Jesus Christ," he is passionate about seeing lives restored and transformed as God intended from the beginning of creation. He has a zeal for the full counsel of the Word of God, fellowship with the Holy Spirit, and being under spiritual authority.

He spearheads the Hour of Meditation Movement, a weekly session dedicated to fostering intimacy, salvation, and the manifestation of miracles in people's lives. Additionally, he organizes numerous "Come and See" Conferences to reach out to lost souls and guide them toward Jesus Christ.

He authored the books *"Now That You Are Born Again, What Next?"*, *"The Blessings of Being Under Spiritual Authority," "A Disciplined Life," "The Enlightened Believer," "The Skilled Sower,"* and other impactful titles. He has also released an album titled *"Divine Encounter"* and many more on the way.

Emmanuel Adewusi is joyfully married to his wife, Ibukun Adewusi, and together, they are building a thriving Christ-centered family.

www.ingramcontent.com/pod-product-compliance
Lightning Source LLC
Chambersburg PA
CBHW070336010526
44107CB00004B/529